The Alchemy of Perception

Change the Way YOU See *Everything*

John Harper

Copyright © 2025 by John Harper

All rights reserved. No part of this publication may be reproduced, distributed, or transmitted in any form or by any means, including photocopying, recording, or other electronic or mechanical methods, without the prior written permission of the publisher, except in the case of brief quotations embodied in critical reviews and specific other noncommercial uses permitted by copyright law. First Edition: September 2025

ISBN: 979-8-9924438-7-5 (Paperback)

HarpGnosis Books

Dedicated to

The Flame that Seeks and the Light that Reveals—this book bows to that ancient movement within us that will not rest until it knows—to the quiet fire that burns through illusion, asking not for comfort but for clarity. To the unseen radiance that waits behind every perception, illuminating even our blindness with its patient grace. This work is for that living mystery—the ever-seeking, ever-revealing dance through which awareness discovers itself in form, loses itself in wonder, and finds itself again as the very light it was searching for.

Prelude

The Many Eyes of Seeing

Every alchemy begins with a base element. In this work, that element is perception—the ordinary way we encounter the world through our senses and minds. At first, perception seems simple: the eye sees, the ear hears, the mind interprets. Yet beneath this everyday act lies a deeper mystery.

Consciousness has never lost contact with its light. What appears as the outer world is that same light refracted through form. The journey of perception is not about discovering the light, but rediscovering that it was never absent. You could say that external consciousness—awareness turned outward through the senses—slowly rediscovers its source, the inner radiance from which all perception arises. The veil lifts, and what seemed divided reveals itself as one seamless field of knowing.

Ordinarily, we think of perception as a taking in—as if the senses gather information and deliver it to the mind for interpretation. But from the perspective of consciousness, perception is not an act of intake—it is an act of intimacy. It is not the movement of the world entering us, but of awareness entering itself.

We might say that alchemical perception is not passive reception but active penetration—a dynamic participation in the unfolding of being. It is not about grasping the world but being entered by it, a meeting so complete that no boundary remains between perceiver and perceived.

Ordinary perception functions like consumption—the world enters us through the senses, and the mind digests it into meaning. However, in truth, perception is not the consumption of reality; it is an active participation in it. Awareness does not stand apart and receive—it enters, communes, and merges. True seeing is not an act of acquisition but of surrender. Perception is not how we take in the world; it is how the world comes alive within us as itself. In this sense, perception is not the bridge between self and world, but rather the realization that no such bridge was ever needed.

This prelude begins that transformation.

When we use the word seeing in this book, we do not mean sight alone. We mean the whole act of consciousness perceiving itself through the senses. The eyes are only one aperture in a larger body of awareness. To see in this deeper sense is to touch, hear, taste, and feel the presence of what is before thought has named it. It is the way awareness meets the world—directly, before interpretation.

Pure perception is the undivided immediacy of experience. It does not yet distinguish between inner and outer, between one sense and another. In that instant before thought divides the field, perception is whole—an indivisible intimacy between being and knowing.

Here we encounter two movements within perception55555555: apprehension and recognition.

Apprehension arises first. The Latin ad + prehendere means "to grasp toward." Apprehension is the initial contact, the living edge where consciousness touches what is. It is pre-conceptual, pre-verbal—the knowing that trembles at the moment of contact. Before we know what something is, we apprehend its being: the cool air brushing the skin, the vibration of sound before the ear tells us its source, the glimmer of presence before meaning forms. Apprehension is the spark of direct perception—immediate, alive, unmediated.

Then, almost imperceptibly, recognition follows. From the Latin re + cognoscere, "to know again." Recognition is retrospective. It folds the new experience into the pattern of memory. The mind says, This I know. It stabilizes perception by connecting it to the past—naming, identifying, re-knowing. Recognition provides coherence, but it also begins to veil immediacy.

Pure perception is what is before this veiling. It is apprehension without the overlay of recognition—experience unmediated by the mind's archive. It is not anti-cognitive, but prior to cognition, the raw gold of awareness, before it is alloyed with meaning.

In alchemical language, perception is the crucible; apprehension is the fire that ignites the transformation, and recognition is the condensation of vapor into form. Each is necessary, yet the alchemist of perception learns to stay with the fire—to remain in the heat of direct apprehension without rushing to cool it into recognition.

But where does this alchemy occur? Not in the intellect. Not in the sensory apparatus. It takes place in the heart—the true crucible of transformation.

The mind observes, the senses report, but the heart knows. The heart is not sentimental or emotional in this context; it is the luminous center of being, the organ of truth. It is where awareness and love converge, where knowing and being are one movement. In the heart, perception is experienced as intimacy, not distance. What is seen is not apart from the seer—it is experienced as oneself: ipseity, the pure presence of being aware of being.

All true knowing is heart-knowing. The heart is where apprehension deepens into communion and where recognition becomes remembrance of unity rather than repetition of the past. It is within this inner chamber that perception is purified, where the dross of interpretation burns away, and what remains is the direct radiance of truth.

When we speak of seeing, then, we speak of this state: the immediacy of awareness before the mind recognizes, and the intimacy of the heart knowing what is. Seeing is the pure act of apprehending reality through all senses at once, before the division into seeing, hearing, touching, or knowing occurs.

In this light, pure perception is not a refinement of the senses but the dissolution of their separateness. It is the return of the five streams into one current—the one eye through which consciousness knows itself. Recognition has its place; it organizes the world. But apprehension reveals the world's living truth. One recalls the past; the other unveils the present. In the alchemy of perception, both are transmuted. Recognition becomes transparent, serving rather than obscuring apprehension. Seeing becomes knowing, and knowing becomes being.

Pure perception is not about what you look at, but about what looks through you. It is not the eye that sees, but the light knowing itself within the crucible of the heart.

Rumi speaks of the heart as the secret furnace of the world: all change, all alchemy begins here.

Let's begin where we normally do – at the beginning, which is in the middle of our stream of experience.

Contents

Preface i
Introduction iv
Perception & Awareness 1
    Spring — The Birth of Seeing 1
    Summer — The Fire of Inquiry 5
    Autumn — The Turning of Perspective 8
    Winter — The Stillness of Awareness 11
Identity & Inner Narrative 15
    Spring — The Birth of Story 15
    Summer — The Mirror of Self 19
    Autumn — The Revision of Meaning 22
    Winter — The Disappearance of the Author 25
Emotion & Energy 29
    Spring — The Awakening of Feeling 29
    Summer — The Flow of Energy 32
    Autumn — The Refinement of Feeling 35
    Winter — The Stillness of the Heart 37
The Body as Ground 40
    Spring — Awakening to Embodiment 40
    Summer — The Fire of Sensation 43
    Autumn — The Integration of Form, ...45
    Winter — The Stillness of Flesh 47
Relationship & Belonging 50
    Spring — The Opening of Connection 50
    Summer — The Fire of Intimacy 53
    Autumn — The Mirror of Projection 55
    Winter — The Communion of Being 58

Shadow & Wholeness 61
    Spring — Meeting What Was Cast Away 61
    Summer — The Fire of Integration 64
    Autumn — The Collective Shadow 67
    Winter — The Luminous Dark 70

The Mind's Mirror 74
    Spring — The Awakening of Thought 74
    Summer — The Fire of Mind 77
    Autumn — The Space Between 79
    Winter — The Mirror of Mind 81

Meaning & Purpose 84
    Spring — The Seed of Wonder 84
    Summer — The Fire of Direction 87
    Autumn — The Revision of Story 89
    Winter — The Stillness of Being 91

The River of Becoming 94
    Spring — Awakening to Flow 94
    Summer — The Fire of Choice 97
    Autumn — The Weaving of Destiny 99
    Winter — The Eternal Now 101

The Dance of Opposites 104
    Spring — Opening to Paradox 104
    Summer — The Fire of Integration 107
    Autumn — Holding the Tension 109
    Winter — Beyond Duality 111

The Door with No Key 114
    Spring — The Paradox of Effort 114
    Summer — The Flow of Being 117
    Autumn — The Trust of Surrender 119
    Winter — The Simplicity of What Is 121

The Eye That Sees Itself 124
    Spring — Awareness of Awareness 124

- Summer — The Light of Recognition 127
- Autumn — The Dissolution of Division 129
- Winter — The Silence Beyond Seeing 131qazz

The Transparent Circle 134
- Spring — The Gateless Gate 134
- Summer — The Fire of Dissolution 137
- Autumn — The Integration of Nothing 139
- Winter — The Breath of Silence 141

The Circle Breathes You 145
The Soul as the Lens of the Absolute 146
52 Lenses 147
The Inner Architecture Trilogy 150
About the Author 152

Preface

You are holding a book that wants to disappear.

Not because it lacks substance, but because its substance is you—the awareness reading these words, the presence animating your breath, the seeing that happens before thought names what is seen.

> *We live in a world of mystery, wonder, and beauty. But most of us seldom participate in this real world, being aware rather of a world that is mostly strife, suffering, or meaninglessness. This situation is basically due to our not realizing and living our full human potential. This potential can be actualized by the realization and development of the human Essence. The human Essence is the part of us that is innate and real, and can participate in the real world.*

Thus begins **Diamond Heart Book I: Elements of the Real in Man** by A. H. Almaas.

The **Alchemy of Perception** is written in that same spirit—as an invitation to participate fully, consciously, and creatively in the real world, to change the way you see everything. This is not a book about accumulating knowledge but about transforming the instrument through which all knowing occurs: perception.

The mystics called this "polishing the mirror of the heart." Modern neuroscience now confirms what contemplatives have always known: **the quality of consciousness shapes the reality we experience.** Change how you see, and the world transforms—not metaphorically, but actually.

For millennia, seekers across traditions have pursued this alchemy. The Desert Fathers sat in silence until the veil between seen and unseen thinned. Zen monks faced walls until the walls dissolved into vastness. Ibn Arabi described ascending through seven heavens of meaning, each unveiling a subtler perception of Reality. The anonymous author of *The Cloud of Unknowing* urged practitioners to "strike down every clever thought beneath a cloud of forgetting," for true knowing arises only when the mind's scaffolding collapses.

Each of these practices was not a retreat from life but a reorientation of seeing—an inner refinement through which the ordinary reveals its hidden radiance.

Today, we stand at a threshold. Neuroscientists map the brain's correlates of mystical insight. Psychologists study ego dissolution. Researchers explore how psilocybin, MDMA, and other entheogens induce shifts in perception, meaning, and relationship that can endure long after the experience fades. These are not chemical curiosities—they are modern doorways into ancient questions:

- *What is consciousness?*
- *What is reality when the self disappears?*
- *What remains when perception is freed from habitual filters?*

Studies reveal that such experiences—whether through contemplative practice, crisis, nature, or entheogens—lead to enduring transformation, characterized by greater empathy, connectedness, openness, and a sense of unity that transcends fear and division. Neural imaging shows that the boundaries of self loosen as brain regions synchronize into broader coherence. It is as if the human system, when freed from contraction, remembers its original symmetry with Being.

This book is a manual for that remembrance.

It offers fifty-two lenses—one for each week of the year—each designed not to teach *what* to see, but to refine *how* seeing happens. Each lens shifts the angle of perception, revealing how assumptions, reactions, and judgments shape experience. To look through these lenses is to enter the ancient practice of contemplation, where perception becomes both crucible and gold.

The aim is not transcendence but participation: to live awake within the mystery that has always been here. This alchemy requires neither monasteries, psychedelics, nor mountain caves—only sincerity of attention and willingness to question what you believe is real.

Every breakthrough, whether in a monastery or a laboratory, begins when perception dissolves its certainty. When seer and seen are no longer separate, perception becomes revelation. And through that revelation, the ordinary world—

this very moment—becomes the philosopher's stone, transforming everything it touches into light.

May these contemplations serve as your crucible for that light.

John Harper
Folsom, California
November 2025

Introduction

The World You See Is the World You Create

Stand at a window and look outside.

What do you see? Trees, sky, perhaps the movement of clouds or the stillness of stone. But here is what you do not see: the vast filtering system operating between the world and your awareness of it.

Your sensory systems take in millions of bits of data every second, but your conscious mind can attend to only a few dozen of them—an infinitesimal fraction of what you perceive. Everything else is discarded, edited, translated through memory, expectation, fear, and desire before it reaches what you call "seeing."

You are not perceiving reality. You are perceiving a highly curated translation of reality—one shaped by biology, conditioning, and the stories you've told yourself about who you are.

This is how ordinary human consciousness works. But it becomes a prison when you forget that perception is interpretive, not objective. When you mistake the map for the territory, the menu for the meal, the word for the thing itself.

Perception as Creation

The mystics understood this millennia before neuroscience proved it. What you perceive, you help create. Not through fantasy or imagination, but through the selective focus of attention. Where awareness rests, energy flows. Where energy flows, form appears.

This is not solipsism—the world exists independently of your perception. But your experience of the world does not. Two people can stand at the same window and see entirely different realities: one sees beauty, the other sees threat. Same window. Different worlds.

The difference is not in the window. It is in the perceiver.

The Alchemy of Seeing

Alchemy was, at first, a physical art. The ancient alchemists worked with metals, minerals, and fire—real laboratories filled with crucibles, fumes, and furnaces. They sought to purify matter, to discover the laws of transformation hidden within nature. Yet in doing so, they were also—perhaps unknowingly—mirroring an inner process. The transmutation of lead into gold became a living symbol of consciousness refining itself.

Over time, the laboratory moved inward. The fire became inquiry. The vessel became the heart. The elements became qualities of awareness—lead as the heaviness of identification, mercury as fluid consciousness, gold as incorruptible presence. The true alchemist discovered that the experiment and the experimenter were never separate.

This book continues that lineage. Each of the fifty-two lenses you will encounter is a small alchemical operation. Each dissolves a habitual way of perceiving and reveals a clearer one. Some lenses widen awareness; others sharpen it. Some illuminate what was hidden; others dissolve what seemed solid.

All of them share one aim: to help you see that you are not the one who perceives—you are the awareness in which perception unfolds. That shift—from being the seer to realizing yourself as the seeing—is the essence of awakening.

Perception is the process by which consciousness becomes aware of phenomena. It involves the reception, organization, and interpretation of sensory information, but more fundamentally, it is the meeting point between the perceiver and the perceived—the interface through which reality becomes experience.

Philosophically, perception is not merely the passive registration of data; it is a creative act in which meaning is born. It weaves together sensation, memory, emotion, and expectation into a coherent field of awareness. In this sense, perception is participatory—it is how the world and the self come into being for one another.

In psychology, perception is often described as the brain's way of constructing reality from sensory input—filtering, prioritizing, and interpreting stimuli. In contemplative traditions, however, perception is viewed as a direct expression of consciousnesst, unmediated by conceptual thought when it is purified.

In essence: Perception is the bridge between Being and world—where awareness turns into knowing, and knowing gives shape to experience.

The Architecture of This Book

Thirteen domains. Four seasons each. Fifty-two lenses total—one for every week of the year, though you need not follow that rhythm.

Each domain explores a fundamental dimension of human experience:

1. **How we see** (Perception & Awareness)
2. **Who we think we are** (Identity & Inner Narrative)
3. **What moves through us** (Emotion & Energy)
4. **How we inhabit form** (The Body as Ground)
5. **How we meet others** (Relationship & Belonging)
6. **What we reject** (Shadow & Wholeness)
7. **How we think** (The Mind's Mirror)
8. **Why we search** (Meaning & Purpose)
9. **How we move through time** (The River of Becoming)
10. **How we hold paradox** (The Dance of Opposites)
11. **How effort dissolves** (The Door With No Key)
12. **How awareness knows itself** (The Eye That Sees Itself)
13. **How everything returns** (The Transparent Circle)

Within each domain, four seasonal lenses trace the arc of transformation:

- **Spring — Opening:** fresh seeing, curiosity awakening
- **Summer — Illumination:** clarity burning through obscuration
- **Autumn — Integration:** opposites reconciling, wisdom ripening
- **Winter — Dissolution:** form releasing back into essence

This seasonal rhythm mirrors both nature's cycle and consciousness's movement: every insight must open, blaze, integrate, and dissolve before the next can emerge.

How to Work with This Book

There are two ways to move through these lenses:

1. **Sequential practice**: Begin with Domain One, Spring, and move week by week through the year. This builds systematically, each lens preparing the ground for the next.
2. **Intuitive practice**: Open to the domain that calls you now. If relationship troubles you, enter Domain Five. If you're lost in thought, try Domain Seven. Let resonance guide you.

Either way, the work is the same: read the lens slowly, then live it. Not as technique, but as a way of seeing. Allow it to reorient your perception until the shift becomes natural.

The Architecture of Each Lens

Every lens is composed of three elements working together:

- **Mental Model** - A principle or concept that frames perception
- **Thinking System** - A way of moving attention or processing experience
- **Framework** - A practice or structure from wisdom traditions

These three elements combine to create a perceptual shift—a new way of seeing that dissolves habitual patterns and reveals what was hidden.

Lens of Perception

Mental Model + Thinking System + Framework = Lens of Perception

Field of Awareness

Field of Awareness

Mental Model — a principle that reveals how perception works.

Thinking System — the movement that refines perception.

Framework — a structure that brings awareness into embodied practice.

Together, these form a triad of transformation: principle, process, and embodiment.

Field of Awareness

Field of Awareness

How Each Lens Is Explored

Once the lens is introduced, you'll engage it through four movements:

- **The Teaching** - How the three elements weave together into a coherent way of seeing
- **Phenomenological Pointers** - Direct instructions for experiencing this lens in your body and awareness
- **Applications** - How this lens lives in daily life, relationship, and inner work
- **A Koan** - One question or statement to carry as you practice

The lens itself is the perceptual instrument. The four movements teach you how to look through it.

What matters is this: do not try to master these lenses intellectually. Let them work on you the way light works on film—through exposure, not effort.

A Note on Language

This book draws from many traditions—Vedanta, Buddhism, Taoism, Christian mysticism, Sufism, phenomenology, depth psychology, and modern neuroscience. But it belongs to none of them exclusively.

I am not teaching the Diamond Approach, though that path informs my seeing. I am not teaching the Enneagram, though it appears as one lens among many. I am not teaching Buddhism, Christianity, or any single system.

I am pointing toward direct experience—the immediate, wordless knowing that precedes and transcends all systems. Every tradition I reference is a finger pointing at the moon. Don't mistake the finger for the light.

The Diminishing Word

As you progress through this book, you will notice the lenses growing shorter. This is not laziness—it is the teaching.

At first, more scaffolding is needed. The mind must learn to recognize its patterns, to see how perception shapes experience. But as clarity deepens, less needs to be said. The latter domains are intentionally sparse. By then, you will not need my voice—you will have become your own oracle.

The final lens of the final domain is nearly silent. Not because there is nothing left to say, but because by then, the saying and the seeing will have merged.

An Invitation

You are about to enter the phenomenology of perception—the direct study of how awareness manifests as experience. This is not abstract philosophy. It is a living, experiential, phenomenological inquiry.

Each lens will ask you to pause, to notice, to feel into the texture of seeing itself. Not what you see, but the act of seeing. Not what you think, but the space in which thought appears. Not who you are, but the awareness that knows "I AM."

This work will undo you. It will dissolve certainty and replace it with wonder. It will strip away the familiar until only the real remains.

Commit at least one week to exploring each lens before moving on to the next. This is alchemy, not learning.

If you are ready for that—if you can bear the loss of what you thought was true in exchange for what is actually here—then turn the page.

The first domain awaits.

Domain One

Perception & Awareness

The Art of Seeing

Before there is thought, there is seeing. Before meaning arises, there is the bare fact of awareness meeting phenomenon—light touching the eye, sound entering the ear, sensation appearing in the body.

This domain is the foundation of all that follows. Here you learn to distinguish between perception and interpretation, between the immediacy of experience and the stories woven around it. You discover that what you call "reality" is not what appears, but how appearance is met.

The art of seeing is not about seeing better—sharper, clearer, more. It is about seeing freshly, before habit interprets, before memory compares, before the mind names what the senses receive.

In this domain, awareness turns back on itself and discovers the space between stimulus and response—the gap where freedom lives. When you learn to rest in that gap, perception becomes revelation. The world does not change; the one who sees it does.

Spring — The Birth of Seeing

The Season of Opening

Spring is the awakening to perception—the moment you notice that seeing is not passive reception but active creation. The mind does not merely record reality; it organizes, filters, and interprets it according to patterns laid down over years of conditioning.

This lens invites you to loosen those patterns, to see before naming, to meet the world as if for the first time. The goal is not better seeing, but beginner's seeing—fresh, open, uncluttered by conclusion.

The Triadic Lens

- **The Map Is Not the Territory**

  Everything you perceive is a representation, not the thing itself. Your beliefs about reality are maps—useful for navigation, but not to be confused with the terrain. The word *tree* is not the tree. The concept *self* is not the self. All knowledge is symbolic, pointing toward experience but never containing it.

  When you recognize this, perception softens. You stop defending your maps and become curious about the territory beyond them.

- **Beginner's Mind**

  In Zen, *shoshin*—beginner's mind—is the capacity to meet each moment without preconception. It does not mean ignorance; it means presence unburdened by the past. The expert sees what he expects to see. The beginner sees what is actually there.

  Beginner's mind interrupts the reflex to categorize. It creates a pause between perception and interpretation, allowing awareness to breathe.

- **The GROW Model**

  Borrowed from coaching but repurposed here as contemplative inquiry:

  - **Goal**: What do I want to see more clearly?
  - **Reality**: What is actually present, before interpretation?
  - **Options**: What opens when I look from a different angle?
  - **Way Forward**: What will I carry from this seeing into life?

  GROW is not problem-solving; it is phenomenological mapping—moving from intention through immediacy to insight.

Experiencing the Lens

Sit somewhere you know well—a room you inhabit daily. Now look at it as if you've never been here before.

Do not name what you see. Do not recall associations or project meaning. Simply let light, color, and form register without commentary. When the mind moves to label—*chair, window, wall*—notice the labeling and return to pure seeing.

Feel how different this is from ordinary perception. Ordinary seeing is swift, automatic, and designed for survival. This seeing is slow, receptive, and designed for presence.

Notice what happens in the body when you see this way. There is often a softening—the shoulders drop, the breath deepens. Perception without interpretation is restful.

Now stand and walk through the room. Let awareness rest in the sensations of movement—the weight shifting foot to foot, the air against skin, the subtle adjustments of balance. When thought arises (*I should clean this room, I need to call someone*), acknowledge it as thought appearing within awareness, then return to the immediacy of sensation.

This is the practice: over and over, returning to what is actually here before the mind translates it into meaning.

Applications

- **In Daily Life**: Choose one routine activity—washing dishes, walking to the car, making coffee—and do it with beginner's mind. Notice everything as if it were the first time. The temperature of water. The weight of the cup. The sound of your own footsteps. Let the familiar become strange.
- **In Relationship**: Listen to someone speak without preparing your response, without agreeing or disagreeing, without comparing their experience to yours. Just listen as if you've never heard language before—pure sound carrying meaning you're receiving fresh.
- **In Inner Work**: When a familiar emotion arises—anxiety, irritation, longing—meet it without the story. Don't ask why it's here or what it means. Feel it as pure sensation: tightness in the chest, heat in the face, hollowness in the belly. Let the map (the name *anxiety*) drop away and experience the territory (the actual felt sense).

The Koan

What remains when the name is forgotten?

Summer — The Fire of Inquiry

The Season of Illumination

Beginner's seeing is a return to apprehension before recognition—to that living edge where perception touches what is, before the mind divides it into known and unknown.

Summer brings the heat of questioning—the refusal to accept appearances at face value. If Spring showed you to see freshly, Summer teaches you to see critically, to examine the structures of perception.

This is not cynicism but discernment. You begin to notice how expectations shape experience, how beliefs create evidence to support themselves, and how the mind selectively attends to what confirms its existing narrative.

The fire of inquiry burns through lazy perception. It demands:

- Is this true?
- How do I know?
- What am I not seeing?

The Triadic Lens

- **The Observer Effect**

    From quantum physics: the act of observation changes what is observed. The same is true of consciousness. When you look at something with fear, fear shapes what appears. When you look with curiosity, it reveals previously hidden aspects. You are not a neutral witness. Your presence in the field alters the field. Awareness is participatory, not passive.

- **Critical Thinking**

    The discipline of examining assumptions, testing evidence, and recognizing bias. Applied to perception, critical thinking asks:

    - What filters am I seeing through?
    - What do I take for granted?
    - Where am I confusing interpretation with fact?

This is not intellectual analysis—it is embodied discernment. You feel where perception tightens around belief and gently loosen it.

- **The Socratic Method**

    The ancient practice of inquiry through questioning. Rather than asserting what is true, you ask:

    - What do I actually know?
    - How do I know it?
    - Could this be otherwise?

    The Socratic method does not seek answers; it seeks clarity. Each question dissolves a layer of assumption until what remains is direct experience, free of overlay.

Experiencing the Lens

Bring to mind a strong belief you hold—about yourself, about others, about how life works. It doesn't need to be profound; even "I'm not a morning person" will do.

Now interrogate it:

- How do I know this is true?
- What evidence supports it—and what contradicts it?
- When did I first believe this?
- What would change if this belief dissolved?

As you question, notice what happens in the body. Beliefs are not just mental—they live in muscle tension, breathing patterns, gut sensations. When you challenge a belief, you often feel resistance: tightness, heat, a pulling away.

This is the body defending its map. Stay with the questioning anyway. Not to destroy the belief, but to see it clearly as a belief—a working hypothesis, not an absolute truth.

Now move into direct perception. Look at something simple—a plant, a stone, your own hand. Notice when the mind moves to *knowing: This is a fern, it needs water, I should repot it.* Each thought is a layer of interpretation covering the thing itself.

Ask: *What is this before I name it?* Let the layers of knowing peel away until only presence remains—awareness meeting form without conclusion.

Applications

- **In Daily Life**: When you find yourself certain of something, pause. Ask: *What if I'm wrong? What am I not seeing?* Not to destabilize yourself, but to create space for reality to surprise you.
- **In Relationship**: Notice when you think you know what someone is feeling or why they behaved as they did. Test your assumption: "I imagine you're feeling frustrated—is that true?" Often, you'll discover your interpretation was a projection.
- **In Inner Work**: When a judgment arises—about yourself, about an experience—question it. *Who says this is bad? According to what standard? What if this, too, belongs?* Let inquiry soften the edges of your inner critic.

The Koan

How does my seeing shape what I see?

Autumn — The Turning of Perspective

The Season of Integration

Autumn is the season of harvest—gathering the insights of Spring and Summer into embodied wisdom. You have learned to see freshly and question deeply. Now you learn to shift your perspective at will, recognizing that every view is partial and that wholeness emerges through holding multiple views simultaneously.

This is cognitive flexibility—the capacity to reframe experience, to turn it in the light until new facets appear. What seemed solid reveals itself as fluid; what seemed fixed shows its contingency.

The Triadic Lens

- **Cognitive Reframing**

    The recognition that the frame determines the picture. Change the frame, and the same facts appear differently. A setback becomes a lesson. A loss becomes a release. The reframe does not deny reality; it reveals aspects of reality that the original frame obscured.

    Reframing is not positive thinking—it is perceptual alchemy. You are not pretending difficulty is easy; you are seeing difficulty from a wider vantage.

- **Metacognitive Reflection**

    The capacity to observe your thinking as it happens. Metacognition is awareness watching the mind—not getting lost in thought, but noticing: *Ah, judging. Ah, planning. Ah, remembering.*

    When you cultivate this witness, you stop being the thought and become the space in which thought occurs. This creates freedom.

- **Phenomenological Reduction (Epoché)**

    From the philosopher Husserl: the practice of suspending judgment and returning to the phenomenon as it appears before interpretation. You "bracket" your assumptions—set them aside temporarily—to experience what is actually present.

Epoché is radical empiricism. You trust only what is presented directly, without explanation or theory. This does not mean abandoning knowledge; it means loosening its grip so fresh seeing can occur.

Experiencing the Lens

Think of a recent situation that troubled you—an argument, a disappointment, a moment of shame. Notice how you've been holding it in your mind: the frame you've placed around it.

Now reframe it. Not to deny what happened, but to see it from a different angle:

- If this were happening *for* you rather than *to* you, what might it be teaching?
- If you saw this through the eyes of compassion rather than judgment, how would it appear?
- If you stepped back a year from now and looked at this moment, what would matter most?

Feel how the reframe shifts something in the body. The chest opens slightly. The jaw unclenches. Perspective itself is physiological—it changes how energy moves through you.

Now practice epoché. Choose an object nearby—a cup, a book, a stone. Look at it and consciously suspend everything you know about it. Forget its name, its function, its history. See it as pure form: color, texture, light, and shadow.

This is strangely difficult. The mind resists unknowing. But stay with it. Let the object become luminous with presence, seen as if for the first time—yet now you are bringing all your awareness to that first seeing.

Applications

- **In Daily Life**: When stress arises, pause and reframe. *What if this deadline is an invitation to focus? What if this conflict is showing me where I need to clarify boundaries?* The reframe does not remove the challenge; it transforms your relationship to it.
- **In Relationship**: Practice seeing the person before you as if you've never met them. Bracket your history together—the disappointments, the expectations, the roles you've assigned. Who are they, right now, in this moment?
- **In Inner Work**: When you encounter an inner part you dislike—the anxious one, the harsh one, the needy one—practice epoché. Suspend

judgment. Meet this aspect of yourself as pure phenomenon. What does it feel like? What is it trying to protect? Often, what seemed like an enemy reveals itself as an ally.

The Koan

Who am I before the story begins?

Winter — The Stillness of Awareness

The Season of Dissolution

Winter is the season of return—the settling of perception back into its source. You have learned to see more clearly, question more clearly, and reframe more fluidly. Now you learn the deepest art: to rest as the seeing itself, before any object is seen.

This is not a doing but an undoing—the release of effort until only awareness remains. No longer awareness *of* something, but awareness as such: the luminous field in which all perception arises and dissolves.

The Triadic Lens

- **Pure Awareness**

    Consciousness without content. The light by which everything is known, but which cannot itself be seen as an object. You cannot perceive awareness because you *are* awareness—it is the subject that can never become an object.

    Pure awareness is not a state to achieve; it is what you already are, beneath the overlay of thought and sensation. When the mind quiets, awareness reveals itself as the constant background of all experience.

- **Direct Experience**

    The immediacy of contact precedes cognition. Direct experience is pre-verbal, pre-conceptual—sensation meeting awareness without mediation. The warmth of the sun on the skin. The sound of rain on glass. The breath moving in and out.

    In direct experience, there is no distance between knower and known. Subject and object collapse into a single field of presence.

- **Husserl's Epoché (Deepened)**

    The same practice introduced in Autumn, now taken to its natural conclusion. You bracket not only judgments and assumptions but all content—until even the sense of being *someone* perceiving softens.

What remains is awareness aware of itself, the infinite space in which worlds appear and disappear without leaving a trace.

Experiencing the Lens

Sit quietly and allow your body to settle. Feel the weight of sitting, the rhythm of breath, the hum of life in the chest.

Now turn attention toward awareness itself. Not toward what you are aware of, but toward the aware-ing. Who is noticing breath? Who registers sensation?

When you look for this one, you will not find a thing. There is no entity called "the witness." There is only witnessing—a vast openness in which perception occurs.

Rest here. Let thoughts come and go like clouds across the sky. Let sensations rise and fall like waves in an ocean. You are not the clouds or the waves. You are the sky, the ocean—the still expanse that holds everything without being touched by anything.

If you lose yourself in thought, simply notice: *Ah, thinking*. This noticing is already awareness returning to itself. You don't need to force presence; it is always already here. You only need to stop leaving.

Now, let even the sense of observing dissolve. You are not watching awareness—you are *being* awareness. The watcher and the watched are one movement, one light.

Sit in this recognition. It is not a feeling or a vision. It is simpler than anything the mind can grasp: the bare fact of being aware, prior to all content.

When you are ready, open your eyes and let perception return. Notice that awareness does not change. Seeing happens; awareness remains. Sound arises; awareness remains. Thought moves; awareness remains.

You have not gained something new. You have recognized what was always here, so obvious it was overlooked—the simple, radiant fact of being conscious.

Applications

- **In Daily Life**: Throughout the day, pause and notice: *I am aware*. Not "I am aware of this" or "I am aware of that"—just the bare recognition of being awake to experience. This noticing is itself the teaching.
- **In Relationship**: When someone speaks, notice the awareness that receives their words. It is the same awareness in them that is speaking. Two

forms, one light. Let this recognition soften the boundary between self and other.
- **In Inner Work**: When meditation feels dry or effortful, abandon technique. Simply be. Awareness does not need your help to be aware. It is already fully present, fully alive. Your only work is to stop interfering.

The Koan

What sees the seeing?

Closing Reflection on Domain One

Perception is not the window through which you see the world—it is the glass itself, shaping what appears.

Through these four lenses, you have learned:

- To see freshly, before habit interprets (Spring)
- To question deeply, examining the structures of seeing (Summer)
- To reframe fluidly, recognizing all views as partial (Autumn)
- To rest as awareness, the source of all perception (Winter)

Each lens is a loosening—a gentle dissolution of the filters that narrow experience. As perception refines, the world does not become less but *more*: more vivid, more immediate, more mysteriously alive.

This is the beginning of awakening—not a dramatic revelation, but a quiet intimacy with what is. When you see without distortion, the ordinary becomes luminous. Every leaf, every face, every breath shines with the same light: awareness meeting itself in form.

The work of Domain One never ends. No matter how deep your practice grows, you will return here again and again—to the simple art of seeing before knowing, perceiving before naming, being present before becoming someone present.

Let this domain be your foundation. Everything that follows builds on this ground: the recognition that perception is participatory, that awareness shapes experience, and that the world you see is the world you are.

Domain Two

Identity & Inner Narrative

The Stories We Inhabit

Who are you?

Not the social answer—your name, your role, your history. Not even the psychological answer—your personality, your wounds, your gifts. But the living question beneath all answers: who is here, right now, before the story begins?

Most of us live inside a narrative so familiar we mistake it for reality. *I am this kind of person. I've always been this way. This is just how I am.* The story feels solid, unchangeable, true. But it is not truth—it is interpretation solidified through repetition.

This domain explores the architecture of identity: how the sense of self is woven from memory, perception, and language; how narrative gives coherence to the chaos of experience; and how the one you take yourself to be is both a necessary fiction and an ultimate obstacle.

The work here is delicate. You are not trying to destroy the self—that would be another story, another strategy of the ego. You are learning to see it clearly: identity as process, not substance; story as movement, not monument.

When awareness sees the self as a construction, something profound occurs. The story continues—you still have a name, a history, a way of moving through the world—but you are no longer imprisoned by it. The narrative becomes transparent, and through that transparency, freedom appears.

Spring — The Birth of Story

The Season of Becoming

Spring in the life of identity is the moment you recognize: *I am not my story—I am the one telling it.*

This is both relief and vertigo. If the self is not fixed, who are you? The question opens like a chasm, and the mind rushes to fill it with new answers, better stories. But the real invitation is to remain in the opening—to feel what it's like when identity loosens its grip.

Every child constructs a self. It begins innocently: the world responds to your cry, and you learn *I am someone who affects things.* You are praised for being smart, scolded for being loud, and the pattern crystallizes: *I am the smart one. I am too much.* Over time, these fragments coalesce into "me"—a coherent story that makes life navigable.

But what was once fluid hardens into fact. The story becomes the prison.

The Triadic Lens

- **Constructivism**

    Knowledge is not discovered; it is constructed. The ego self is no different. What you call "I" is a dynamic process—assembled from language, memory, emotion, and the mirror of others' eyes. Identity is an ongoing act of interpretation, not a pre-existing fact.

    Constructivism reveals that because the self is built, it can be rebuilt. You are not stuck with the story you inherited or the one you've been telling. Awareness can loosen the structure and allow something new to emerge.

- **Reflective Thinking**

    The capacity to observe your thought process as it unfolds. When you reflect, you step back from identification and notice: *Ah, this is a thought about who I am, not who I actually am.*

    Reflective thinking creates space between experience and interpretation. In that space, identity becomes visible as construction rather than truth.

- **The Hero's Journey**

    Joseph Campbell's universal pattern: the call to adventure, the descent into the unknown, the discovery of inner resources, the return home transformed. Every life is a mythic journey—whether you recognize it or not.

The Hero's Journey reveals that identity is not static; it is a story in motion. The "you" who began the journey is not the one who returns. Each chapter rewrites the self.

Experiencing the Lens

Sit quietly and ask: *Who am I?*

Do not answer with facts—your name, your occupation, your relationships. Go deeper. Who is the one asking the question?

When an answer arises—*I am a parent, I am anxious, I am someone who tries hard*—notice that this is thought appearing in awareness. You are not the thought. You are the space in which the thought occurs.

Ask again: *Who am I?*

Each answer is another layer of story. Keep going. Peel them back one by one until you reach silence—the vast openness in which all stories arise.

Now, bring to mind your origin story: the narrative you tell about how you became who you are. Perhaps it involves childhood wounds, pivotal moments, and turning points. Notice how this story organizes your sense of self. It creates coherence: *I am this way because that happened.*

Feel how the body responds to the story. Does it tighten or relax? Does it feel like truth or like armor?

Now, experiment: tell the same events from a different angle. If your story is "I was abandoned and learned not to trust," try "I was released early and learned self-reliance." Not to deny pain, but to notice how the frame shapes identity.

The facts remain the same. The meaning shifts. And with the meaning, the self shifts too.

Applications

- **In Daily Life**: Notice when you introduce yourself—whether out loud or internally. What story do you lead with? *I'm the kind of person who...* Each phrase is identity asserting itself. Pause before the assertion and feel the openness beneath it.
- **In Relationship**: When someone asks, "What do you do?" resist the reflex to define yourself by role. Answer honestly, but notice the impulse to

become the story you're telling. You are not your job, your status, your accomplishments—you are the awareness that flows through all of them.

- **In Inner Work**: Journal your origin story, then rewrite it from three different perspectives: as tragedy, as comedy, as myth. Notice how each version reveals something true while none contains the whole truth. This is the fluidity of identity.

The Koan

Who am I before the story begins?

Summer — The Mirror of Self

The Season of Reflection

Summer brings the recognition that identity is not self-generated—it is co-created. You become who you are through the eyes of others: parents, teachers, lovers, culture. The self is a hall of mirrors, each reflection shaping how you see yourself.

This is both humbling and liberating. If identity is relational, then it can shift as relationships shift. You are not fixed; you are a living response to the field of connection.

The danger is that you mistake the reflection for reality. You become the image others project, forgetting that beneath the reflection is something luminous and unnameable.

The Triadic Lens

- **The Looking-Glass Self**

    Coined by sociologist Charles Cooley: we see ourselves as we imagine others see us. The self is not an internal discovery but a social construction—formed in dialogue, refined through feedback, stabilized through repetition.

    The looking-glass self explains why identity shifts in different contexts. You are one person with your family, another with colleagues, another alone. Each reflection calls forth a different aspect of self.

- **Narrative Thinking**

    The mind organizes experience into story: beginning, middle, end; cause and effect; character and arc. Narrative thinking is how we make sense of chaos—but it also limits perception. Once the story solidifies, we see only what confirms it.

    When you observe narrative thinking as it happens, you begin to see the editing process: what gets included, what gets left out, how memory revises the past to fit the present identity.

- The Enneagram

The Enneagram appears here not as a personality system, but as a map of attention — nine distinct ways consciousness learns to orient to feel safe, valuable, or connected. It shows how identity becomes patterned: where attention habitually goes, what it avoids, and how it organizes experience into a coherent "me."

To apply the Enneagram in this domain, notice how attention behaves in real time. Does it move outward to secure value? Inward to conserve energy? Toward intensity? Toward harmony? Toward certainty? Each movement is a clue. Identity lives inside these micro-movements of attention.

Experiencing the Lens

Think of someone whose opinion of you matters. Now feel into how you imagine they see you. Do they think you're competent? Needy? Strong? Difficult?

Notice how this imagined perception shapes your behavior around them. You may perform competence to confirm their view, or rebel against it to assert autonomy. Either way, their gaze shapes your sense of self.

Now ask: *Is this how they actually see me, or is this my projection?* Often, the mirror you're looking into is your own mind, not theirs.

Feel what happens in the body when you release the need to be seen a certain way. The shoulders drop. The breath deepens. There is relief in letting the image go.

Now bring awareness to your narrative about your life. Notice its arc: *I struggled, then I found my way. I was lost, now I'm found. I used to be X, now I'm Y.*

This narrative is not false—it points to real experience. But it is also selective. It emphasizes certain events and ignores others. It creates a protagonist—"me"—and organizes the story around that character.

What would change if you told the story differently? If the protagonist were not you but life itself, moving through you?

Applications

- **In Daily Life**: Notice how your identity shifts depending on context. At work, you may be confident and decisive. At home, vulnerable and uncertain. Neither is false; both are partial. The question is: who are you when no one is watching?

- **In Relationship**: Pay attention to how you adjust yourself to be seen in certain ways. Not to judge this—it's natural. However, note the energy it takes to maintain the image. What would it feel like to be seen as you are, without performance?
- **In Inner Work**: Explore your Enneagram type—not to label yourself, but to see the pattern of your perceiving. How does your attention habitually move? What do you focus on, and what do you overlook? The pattern is not you; it's how consciousness has learned to organize itself through your life. Seeing it loosens its grip.

The Koan

Who am I when no one is looking?

Autumn — The Revision of Meaning

The Season of Reinterpretation

Autumn in the life of identity is the time of harvest and revision. You have seen that the self is constructed, that identity is mirrored relationally. Now you learn that meaning itself is fluid—and with the shift in meaning, the self transforms.

This is not self-deception or spiritual bypassing. It is the recognition that the same event can carry different meanings depending on how it is held in awareness. A wound can be a limitation or an initiation. A failure can be an ending or a beginning.

When you revise meaning, you revise identity. The one who was broken becomes the one who has depth. The one who was abandoned becomes the one who learns self-reliance, not as a denial of pain, but as an expansion of truth.

The Triadic Lens

- **Cognitive Reframing**

    The same event, held in a different frame, reveals other aspects of reality. Reframing is not positive thinking—it is perceptual flexibility. You are not pretending suffering didn't happen; you are seeing what else is also true.

    When identity is reframed, the past changes—not the facts, but their significance. Memory is not fixed; it is alive, responsive to present awareness.

- **Metacognition**

    Thinking about thinking. When you observe the mind creating meaning, you see the interpretive process in action: *This means I'm unlovable. This means I'm capable. This means life is unfair.*

    Metacognition reveals that meaning is not inherent in events—it is applied by the mind. And what the mind applies, awareness can revise.

- **The Cognitive Triad**

    From cognitive psychology: three lenses through which identity is filtered:

    - View of Self (*I am capable / I am inadequate*)
    - View of World (*Life supports me / Life is hostile*)

- View of Future (*Things will work out / Nothing will change*)

When one of these views shifts, the others reorganize. Change how you see yourself, and the world appears different. Change your view of the future, and present identity transforms.

Experiencing the Lens

Bring to mind a difficult chapter of your life—a time of loss, failure, or confusion. Notice the meaning you've given it: *That was when I learned I wasn't enough. That's when everything fell apart.*

Now gently ask: *What else was happening that I didn't see?* Was there also resilience? Clarity? The beginning of something new, hidden within the ending?

You are not rewriting history. You are allowing the full truth to emerge—not just the story of suffering, but the story of growth that lies hidden within it.

Feel how the body responds to the reframe. There may be a softening, a release of held tension. Meaning is not just mental—it lives in the tissues, the breath, the heart's rhythm.

Now turn attention to the Cognitive Triad. Notice your current view of self, world, and future. Are they generous or harsh? Expansive or contracted?

Choose one and experiment with reframing:

- If you see yourself as inadequate, what evidence contradicts that? When have you been more than enough?
- If you see the world as hostile, where have you been held, supported, surprised by kindness?
- If the future feels closed, what small opening might exist that you haven't noticed?

The reframe is not about forcing optimism. It is about loosening certainty so that reality—which is always more than your interpretation—can reveal itself.

Applications

- **In Daily Life**: When something goes wrong, pause before assigning meaning. Instead of *This is a disaster*, try *This is unexpected. I don't yet know what this means.* Let meaning unfold rather than imposing it immediately.
- **In Relationship**: When someone disappoints you, notice the story you create: *They don't care. They always do this. I can't rely on anyone.* Then reframe:

They're struggling. They forgot. This moment is not the whole story. Not to excuse harm, but to see more fully.
- **In Inner Work**: Revisit a memory you've held as definitive proof of your identity—*This is when I learned I was unworthy*—and ask what else was also true in that moment. Often, the memory that formed identity also contains the seed of its dissolution.

The Koan

What if the story I've been telling is one chapter, not the whole book?

Winter — The Disappearance of the Author

The Season of Dissolution

Winter is the season when the storyteller goes silent. Not because there is nothing left to say, but because saying itself has become transparent. The narrative continues—you still have a name, a life, a way of being in the world—but you are no longer the author. You are the page on which the words appear.

This is not the erasure of self but its transparency. Identity becomes so light, so fluid, that it no longer obscures the awareness beneath it. The self is still here—functional, responsive, alive—but it is no longer solid. It is like a wave that knows itself as the ocean.

The Triadic Lens

- **The Empty Self**

    From Buddhist psychology: the recognition that the self has no inherent, independent existence. What you call "I" is a process, not an entity—a stream of sensations, thoughts, memories, arising and passing in awareness.

    The empty self is not a void. It is openness—the spaciousness in which identity can move freely without crystallizing into fixed form.

- **Paradoxical Thinking**

    The capacity to hold opposites without resolution. You are both someone and no one. The self is both real and illusory. Identity matters and doesn't matter.

    Paradoxical thinking is the hallmark of mature awareness. It does not collapse contradiction into compromise; it allows both truths to coexist.

- **The Nondual View**

    Awareness and identity are not two. The self is not separate from the seeing—it is seeing appearing as form. When this is recognized, identification loosens. You no longer defend the self because you no longer believe it is all you are.

The nondual view does not erase individuality. It reveals that individuality is one movement of the infinite expressing itself.

Experiencing the Lens

Sit quietly and notice the sense of "I." Not the thought *I am this* or *I am that*, but the bare feeling of being someone—the subtle contraction that says *me, here, now*.

Where is it located? In the chest? The head? Everywhere? Nowhere?

When you look for the self directly, it becomes elusive. You find thoughts about the self, sensations associated with the self, memories of the self—but the self itself cannot be grasped.

This is not because it doesn't exist. It is because the self is not a thing—it is a process, a movement of awareness organizing experience into coherence.

Now, rest as the awareness that watches this process. Not as a separate observer, but as the open field in which self-ing occurs. Thoughts arise: *I should... I want... I am...* Each one is identity asserting itself. And each one dissolves back into the silence from which it came.

Notice that awareness lacks an identity. It is simply here—vast, still, untouched by the stories that move through it.

Let the sense of being someone soften. Not through effort, but through recognition: you are not the wave. You are the ocean, briefly taking the shape of a wave.

Applications

- **In Daily Life**: When you catch yourself saying "I am..." pause. Notice that you are identifying with a temporary state, a passing experience. Feel the difference between *I am angry* (identification) and *Anger is present* (awareness). The shift is subtle but liberating.
- **In Relationship**: Notice how much energy goes into defending, explaining, or justifying the self. What would it be like to meet others without the need to be seen as anyone in particular? Not as self-erasure, but as transparency—letting the light shine through without obstruction.
- **In Inner Work**: When meditation feels effortful, it is often because "someone" is trying to meditate. Let that someone dissolve. There is no

meditator, no one getting it right or wrong. There is only awareness, being what it already is.

The Koan

Who remains when the author disappears?

Closing Reflection on Domain Two

Identity is the necessary fiction through which awareness learns itself. Without the story of "me," there would be no learning, no growth, no intimacy with the texture of being human.

But the story is not the truth. It is a lens—useful, even beautiful, but ultimately transparent.

Through these four lenses, you have explored:

- How the self is constructed through story and reflection (Spring)
- How identity forms relationally, shaped by the mirror of others (Summer)
- How meaning can be revised, and with it, the self transformed (Autumn)
- How the author dissolves, leaving only awareness (Winter)

This is not a path of self-destruction but of self-clarification. You do not need to kill the ego; you need to see through it. When identity becomes transparent, it continues to function—but it no longer imprisons.

The one who began this domain is not the one finishing it. Something has loosened. The story feels lighter. And in that lightness, space appears—the freedom to be no one in particular, yet fully present as whoever you are right now.

Let this spaciousness carry you into Domain Three, where emotion and energy reveal themselves not as obstacles to awakening, but as its embodiment.

Domain Three

Emotion & Energy

The Weather of the Soul

Emotion is not a problem to be solved. It is energy moving through the body—life expressing itself in waves of sensation that carry intelligence the mind alone cannot access.

Most spiritual teachings treat emotions with suspicion: transcend them, control them, or witness them from a distance. However, this domain invites a different kind of relationship. Here, you learn to feel fully without becoming identified, to let energy move without resistance, and to discover that emotion—when met with awareness—refines into something luminous.

The body is where this alchemy happens. Not in thought, not in understanding, but in the direct experience of sensation: the tightness in the chest when fear arises, the warmth that spreads through the limbs in joy, the heaviness that settles in grief.

Emotion is weather—it comes, it passes, it shapes the landscape of consciousness. You are not the storm. You are the sky that holds it.

Spring — The Awakening of Feeling

The Season of Recognition

Spring begins when you stop fleeing emotion and start feeling it. Not analyzing why it's here or what it means, but experiencing it as sensation—texture, temperature, movement in the body.

This requires courage. The body has learned to numb, to distract, to explain away what it feels. But beneath the numbness is aliveness waiting to be met.

The Triadic Lens

- **Emotional Granularity**

    The capacity to distinguish subtle shades of feeling. Not just "I feel bad" but "I feel disappointed, tender, restless, wistful." Each word opens a different doorway into experience.

    Granularity transforms emotional overwhelm into navigable terrain. When you can name what you feel with precision, the nervous system begins to regulate. The prefrontal cortex comes online, and reactivity softens into response.

- **Experiential Awareness**

    Turning attention toward direct sensation rather than interpretation. Instead of asking *Why am I anxious?*, you ask *Where is anxiety in my body? What does it feel like?*

    Experiential awareness bypasses the story and meets the energy directly. It reveals that emotion is not solid—it moves, shifts, dissolves when allowed.

- **The Window of Tolerance**

    From trauma research: The range of arousal within which you can remain present. Too much activation—panic, rage—and you leave the window into hyperarousal. Too little—numbness, collapse—and you fall into hypoarousal.

    The practice is learning to widen the window: to feel more without fragmenting, to stay embodied through intensity.

Experiencing the Lens

Pause and scan your body. Without labeling or interpreting, notice what sensations are present. Tightness? Warmth? Hollowness? Tingling?

Now bring awareness to an emotion that's been moving through you recently—perhaps something still lingering in the background. Don't name it yet. Just feel where it lives in the body.

Does it have a location? A shape? A temperature? Is it moving or still?

When the mind rushes to explain—*I'm anxious because of the meeting tomorrow*—gently return to the sensation itself. The feeling exists now, in the body, independent of the story.

Now name it. But be precise. Not just "anxious" but "apprehensive and slightly excited" or "restless with a thread of anticipation." Each word you add brings more clarity.

Notice: as you name the feeling accurately, something shifts. The body relaxes slightly. The emotion hasn't disappeared, but your relationship to it has changed. You are no longer lost in it—you are with it.

Applications

- **In Daily Life**: When strong emotion arises, pause before acting. Place a hand on your chest or belly and feel the sensation. Name it aloud or silently. This simple act interrupts reactivity and creates space for choice.
- **In Relationship**: When someone triggers you, notice the body's response before the mind's story. *Heat rising, jaw clenching, breath shortening.* Stay with the sensation long enough for it to settle, then speak from clarity rather than charge.
- **In Inner Work**: Build a vocabulary for feeling. Journal not about why you're sad, but what sadness feels like: heavy, cold, pressing, hollow. The body speaks in sensation; learn its language.

The Koan

What is emotion before I name it?

_____

_____

_____

Summer — The Flow of Energy

The Season of Movement

Summer reveals emotion as energy in motion—not static states but currents moving through the nervous system. When allowed, emotions flow: they rise, peak, and release. When blocked, they stagnate into a mood, symptom, or pattern.

The body knows how to move energy. Tears release grief. Trembling discharges fear. Laughter opens the chest. However, conditioning teaches suppression, and suppression ultimately leads to suffering.

The Triadic Lens

- **Energy Conservation**

   From physics: Energy is never destroyed, only transformed. Emotion that isn't expressed doesn't disappear—it converts into tension, illness, or unconscious behavior. When energy is allowed to complete its movement, the system returns to equilibrium.

- **Embodied Cognition**

   Intelligence is distributed throughout the body. The gut senses danger before the mind is aware of it. The heart recognizes resonance. The shoulders carry unexpressed anger.

   Embodied cognition reminds you that thinking happens everywhere, not just in the head. To understand emotion, you must feel it—not conceptually, but somatically.

- **Polyvagal Theory**

   The nervous system has three primary states: ventral vagal (safe, social, connected), sympathetic (mobilized, activated), and dorsal vagal (shutdown, collapsed). Emotion moves through these states like weather through seasons.

   Regulation is not about staying calm—it's about flowing flexibly between states and returning to presence.

Experiencing the Lens

Stand and notice your breath. Now recall a moment of frustration—something small, recent. Let the memory bring the feeling into the body.

Where does it gather? Shoulders? Jaw? Fists?

Instead of thinking about the frustration, let the body express it through movement. Shake your hands. Stomp your feet. Make sound—a growl, a sigh, whatever wants to emerge.

This may feel strange, even childish. Let it be weird. The body has its own intelligence; trust it.

As you move, notice the energy shifting. What was stuck begins to circulate. The nervous system completes the loop it couldn't complete when the frustration first arose.

After a minute or two, pause. Feel the difference. The emotion hasn't been suppressed or indulged—it's been metabolized. The body is calmer, more present.

Now practice regulation. Sit quietly and place one hand on your heart, one on your belly. Breathe slowly—six seconds in, six seconds out. This activates the ventral vagal system, signaling safety.

Feel how this simple act shifts your internal weather. The body responds to the message: *You are held. You can rest.*

Applications

- **In Daily Life**: When emotion builds, move. Walk, dance, stretch. Energy needs expression; give it a pathway. Even five minutes of conscious movement can transform a stuck feeling into flow.
- **In Relationship**: Notice your nervous system state. Are you activated (sympathetic) or shut down (dorsal)? Before engaging in a difficult conversation, take a moment to regulate. Place both feet on the ground, lengthen your spine, breathe. Connect before you speak.
- **In Inner Work**: Let emotion be physical. If grief arises, let yourself sob—not for catharsis but for completion. If joy arises, let your body express it: open your arms and release your voice. Emotion longs to move; honor its nature.

The Koan

Where does the energy go when I stop holding it?

Autumn — The Refinement of Feeling

The Season of Transmutation

Autumn is the season when raw emotion ripens into essential quality. Anger, fully felt and understood, reveals strength. Fear clarifies into discernment. Grief opens into compassion.

This is the alchemy emotion undergoes when met with awareness—not bypassed, not indulged, but held long enough for its intelligence to reveal itself.

The Triadic Lens

- **Emotional Transmutation**

  From the Diamond Approach and depth psychology, emotion is not just a reaction; it contains essential qualities obscured by conditioning. When felt without defense, emotion refines—base metal becoming gold.

- **Somatic Reflection**

  Contemplating experience through the body's wisdom. Rather than analyzing why you feel something, you reflect on how it feels and what it reveals. The body becomes oracle.

- **The Felt Sense (Gendlin)**

  Eugene Gendlin's discovery: beneath every emotion is a *felt sense*—a subtle, pre-verbal knowing that carries more information than thought alone. When you stay with the felt sense, meaning emerges organically.

Experiencing the Lens

Choose an emotion that visits you often—one you've met many times but perhaps never fully understood. Not the most overwhelming one; something workable.

Sit quietly and invite this feeling into awareness. Let it gather in the body. Notice where it lives, how it moves.

Now ask: *What does this emotion want me to know?*

Don't answer with your mind. Wait. Let the question settle into the body and notice what arises—an image, a word, a shift in sensation. This is the felt sense speaking.

Stay with it. The first answer is often surface. If "I'm sad" arises, ask a deeper question: *What kind of sadness? What is its quality?*

You may discover that what seemed like sadness is actually longing, or tenderness, or grief for something beautiful that has passed. Each layer of feeling, when met with curiosity, reveals depth.

As you stay present with the emotion, notice if it begins to transform. Sometimes anger softens into clarity about boundaries. Sometimes fear reveals the value of what you're protecting. The emotion itself shows you its hidden gift.

Applications

- **In Daily Life**: When the same emotion arises repeatedly, treat it as a teacher. What is it trying to show you? Not in the situation, but about your relationship to life? Let it guide rather than disturb you.
- **In Relationship**: When someone's behavior triggers emotion, pause before reacting. Feel the emotion fully, then ask: *What quality is asking to come forward in me?* Perhaps patience, honesty, or strength. Let the emotion refine into a response rather than a reaction.
- **In Inner Work**: Create a practice of emotional inquiry. Journal not to vent but to listen. Write: "This feeling is..." and let the body complete the sentence. The wisdom is already here; you're learning its language.

The Koan

What gift hides in this feeling?

_____

_____

_____

Winter — The Stillness of the Heart

The Season of Equanimity

The heart, named in the Prelude as the crucible of perception, reveals here its deepest function—not as a feeling organ, but as the field where awareness and love are one act of knowing.

Winter is the season when the heart learns to hold all weather without being moved by it. Not through detachment—this is not coldness—but through spaciousness. Joy and sorrow, fear and peace, pass through like clouds, and the sky remains vast.

This is equanimity: intimacy without clinging, feeling without identification.

The Triadic Lens

- Equanimity

    The balanced heart that remains steady amid change. Not indifference but profound acceptance—the recognition that all emotion is temporary, all energy is movement within stillness.

- Contemplative Awareness

    Resting as the space in which emotion occurs rather than as the one experiencing it. You are not the anger; you are the awareness in which anger appears. This shift is liberation.

- The Heart Sutra

    Form is emptiness, emptiness is form. Emotion is real—feel it fully. And emotion is empty—it has no independent existence. Both are true. When this is seen, nothing disturbs the heart's fundamental peace.

Experiencing the Lens

Sit in stillness and feel your heart—not the physical organ but the energetic center of feeling, the space where emotion is known.

Now imagine this heart as the sky. Emotions are like weather: clouds drifting across, rain falling, and the sun breaking through. The weather changes constantly, but the sky never moves.

Bring to mind a difficult emotion—something present or recent. Let it appear in the sky of your heart. Watch it form, intensify, and begin to dissipate. You are not the emotion. You are the vastness that holds it.

Notice: the heart is never damaged by what passes through it. Joy doesn't inflate it; grief doesn't diminish it. The sky is unchanged by the weather.

Rest here. Let whatever emotion arises be welcome—not because you want it, but because it's already here. Resistance is the only suffering; the feeling itself is just energy in motion.

When you rest as the heart that holds all emotion without preference, something remarkable happens: the emotions don't need to be managed. They regulate themselves. They come when needed, go when complete.

Applications

- **In Daily Life**: When emotion arises, silently acknowledge: *This too.* Not resignation but recognition. This emotion, like all others, is a part of the fullness of being human. Let it be here without needing it to leave.
- **In Relationship**: When someone shares their pain, resist the urge to fix or explain. Simply be the space that holds them. Your equanimity becomes a sanctuary. The steadiness of your presence allows their emotion to unfold completely.
- **In Inner Work**: Let meditation be effortless. You are not trying to create peace or transcend emotion. You are resting as the awareness that is already peaceful, already whole, regardless of what weather moves through.

The Koan

What remains when all weather passes?

_____

_____

Closing Reflection on Domain Three

Emotion is not the enemy of awakening—it is awakening expressing itself through the particular texture of your humanness. When you learn to feel without fleeing, to allow energy to move without resistance, emotion becomes revelation.

Through these lenses, you have discovered:

- How to name feeling with precision, creating space around intensity (Spring)
- How to let energy flow rather than stagnate (Summer)
- How emotion, fully felt, refines into an essential quality (Autumn)
- How the heart holds all feelings without being moved (Winter)

This is not emotional mastery but emotional intimacy—the capacity to be with what is, as it is, without defense or demand.

As you move into Domain Four, you will discover that emotion does not happen *to* the body—it happens *as* the body. The boundary between feeling and form dissolves, and the body reveals itself as the ground of all experience.

Domain Four

The Body as Ground

The Temple of Incarnation

Spirituality often promises transcendence—escape from the body, freedom from the flesh. But the deepest teachings know differently: **the body is not the obstacle to awakening; it is its altar.**

Everything you have explored so far—perception, identity, emotion—happens *through* the body. Without this flesh, there is no experience. Without these senses, no world appears. The body is not a vehicle carrying consciousness; it is consciousness taking shape.

This domain asks you to descend rather than ascend, to discover that the ground beneath your feet is holy ground. Not metaphorically, but phenomenologically. The body you inhabit is the precise form through which the infinite knows itself as the particular, temporary, and alive.

When you truly inhabit the body—not as a concept, but as presence—something extraordinary occurs—the boundary between inner and outer dissolves. The body is revealed not as separate from the world but as the place where world and awareness meet, touch, and become one.

Spring — Awakening to Embodiment

The Season of Descent

Spring in the body begins with a simple recognition: *I am here*. Not "I have a body" but "I am embodied." This shift—from possession to participation—changes everything.

Most of us live slightly outside our bodies, managing them from a distance, treating them as instruments to be controlled. But the body is not an instrument; it is the immediacy of being itself.

The Triadic Lens

- **Somatic Intelligence**

    The body thinks. Not metaphorically—it processes information, makes decisions, and knows things the conscious mind cannot access. The gut senses danger. The heart recognizes resonance. The skin reads atmosphere.

    Somatic intelligence operates beneath language, faster than thought. When you learn to listen to it, the body becomes an oracle rather than an obstacle.

- **Body-Mind Integration**

    Dissolving the false separation between thinking and feeling, mind and flesh. When awareness includes the body fully, cognition becomes embodied: you think with your belly, feel with your spine, and know through sensation.

- **Gurdjieff's Three Centers**

    The intellectual center (head), emotional center (chest), and moving/instinctive center (belly). Most people live overdeveloped in one, atrophied in the others. Balance comes through conscious attention—feeling the body, engaging emotion, letting the mind rest.

Experiencing the Lens

Stop reading and place both feet flat on the floor. Feel the contact—the pressure, temperature, texture. This is not thinking about the feet; this is being the feet, feeling from inside the sensation.

Now bring awareness to your hands. Wiggle your fingers slowly, noticing the movement from within. Not watching your hands move, but feeling the aliveness that moves them.

This is the difference between observing the body and inhabiting it. When you inhabit, there is no distance. You are not looking at the body—you are being the body, feeling it from the inside.

Scan through the body slowly, starting from the head, neck, shoulders, arms, chest, belly, pelvis, legs, and feet. Where is there sensation? Where is there numbness? The numb places are where awareness has withdrawn. Gently invite it back.

Now, notice: most of your mental activity happens in the head—thoughts circling, planning, remembering. What happens if you drop awareness into the belly? Feel the breath there, three fingers below the navel. Let attention settle and notice how thinking slows. The belly is presence; the head is time.

Finally, place one hand on your heart. Feel it beating—this body, alive, now. Not yesterday's body or tomorrow's. This one, pulsing with life you did not create and cannot stop. Let humility soften you. This body is grace.

Applications

- **In Daily Life**: Check in with the body every hour. Stop, feel your feet on the ground, notice your breath. This simple act brings you out of mental abstraction into embodied presence.
- **In Relationship**: When speaking with someone, feel your body as you listen. Notice when you leave—when attention lifts into the head, rehearsing what to say next. Return to the body and listen from there. Presence is somatic.
- **In Inner Work**: Begin meditation not in the breath but in the whole body. Feel the weight of sitting, the temperature of air on skin, the subtle hum of aliveness. Let awareness saturate flesh before it rests as space.

The Koan

Where does awareness end and body begin?

_____

_____

_____

_____

Summer — The Fire of Sensation

The Season of Immediacy

Summer in the body is the recognition that sensation is not secondary to awareness—it *is* awareness taking form. Every touch, taste, sound, scent is consciousness knowing itself through matter.

The senses are not filters obscuring reality; they are reality announcing itself. When you give full attention to sensory experience, the world becomes sacrament.

The Triadic Lens

- **Sensory Gnosis**

  Direct knowing through sensation. Not reasoning toward truth but perceiving it immediately—the warmth of the sun on skin teaching impermanence, the taste of water teaching gift, the texture of breath teaching presence.

- **Phenomenology of the Flesh (Merleau-Ponty)**

  The body is not an object in the world but the perspective from which the world appears. You are not *in* space; you *are* space becoming aware of itself through this particular location, this singular flesh.

- **The Tantric Body**

  In Tantra, the body is cosmos—each chakra a dimension of reality, each sense a doorway to the divine. Matter is not the fallen spirit; it is spirit condensed into form. To fully inhabit the body is to participate in creation.

Experiencing the Lens

Find something to touch—fabric, wood, stone, water. Close your eyes and give it your complete attention. Not the concept of texture but the actual sensation: rough, smooth, warm, yielding.

Let awareness become touch. There is no "you" touching "it"—there is only touching, happening. Subject and object dissolve into pure sensory contact.

Now bring awareness to taste. Place something simple on your tongue—a grape, a sip of water. Do not swallow immediately. Let it rest there. Notice flavor unfolding: sweetness, tartness, complexity. The tongue is an oracle; listen.

Move to sound. Close your eyes and listen to the soundscape around you—near and far, subtle and noticeable. Notice: you do not hear sounds; you *are* the hearing. Awareness and vibration are inseparable.

Finally, open your eyes and look at something beautiful—a flower, a face, light through leaves. See it not as an observer, but as a participant. The seeing and the seen arise together, neither possible without the other.

This is sensory gnosis: knowing through immediate contact, before interpretation. The body is not receiving information about the world—it is the place where the world becomes known.

Applications

- **In Daily Life**: Eat one meal in complete silence, giving full attention to sensation. Taste, texture, temperature, the movement of chewing, the miracle of swallowing. Let the body teach reverence.
- **In Relationship**: Touch becomes sacrament when given full presence. Hold someone's hand and feel the warmth, the pulse, the aliveness meeting aliveness. This is communion.
- **In Inner Work**: Practice sensory meditation. Choose one sense—sound, for example—and rest attention there for ten minutes. Let thought dissolve into pure listening. The senses are doorways; walk through.

The Koan

What does the body know that the mind cannot think?

Autumn — The Integration of Form,

The Season of Coherence

Autumn reveals the body as organized intelligence—not random flesh but a living mandala, each part reflecting the whole, every system in conversation with every other.

When you bring awareness to this coherence, the body becomes your teacher. It shows you balance, rhythm, the dance between stability and change.

The Triadic Lens

- **Embodied Presence**

  The capacity to remain fully in the body while awareness expands beyond it. Not leaving the flesh to touch the infinite, but feeling the infinite through the flesh.

- **Somatic Experiencing**

  Developed by Peter Levine, the body completes what the mind interrupts. Trauma is unfinished movement, emotion is an incomplete gesture. When you allow the body to finish what it started, wholeness returns.

- **The Body as a Mandala**

  In Tibetan Buddhism, the body is sacred geometry—head as crown, heart as lotus, belly as earth. Each center carries specific wisdom. To move through the body is to move through dimensions of reality.

Experiencing the Lens

Stand and feel your posture. Where is there alignment? Where is there collapse or rigidity? The body holds your history—slouched shoulders carry a burden, locked knees resist the flow, a tight jaw guards speech.

Gently adjust: lengthen the spine, soften the knees, release the jaw. Notice how this changes not just the body but consciousness itself. Posture is not cosmetic; it is energetic.

Now bring awareness to the three centers Gurdjieff described:

- The **head center** (forehead, temples): the realm of thought, analysis, planning. Place a hand here and feel its quality—busy, bright, sometimes frantic.
- The **heart center** (chest, between the breasts): the realm of feeling, relationship, resonance. Hand here—notice warmth, openness, or perhaps armor.
- The **belly center** (navel, deep in the abdomen): the realm of instinct, groundedness, power. Hand here—this is your root, your earth.

Most people are overactive in one center, underactive in others. Feel into balance. Let awareness circulate—head to heart to belly and back. The body is not three separate parts but one living whole, each center informing the others.

Applications

- **In Daily Life**: Notice which center you live from most. If you're always in your head, practice dropping into your belly throughout the day—feel your feet and your breath low in the body. If you're always emotional, engage your mind—read, solve a puzzle, or organize something. Balance creates wholeness.
- **In Relationship**: When conflict arises, check in with all three centers. What does your head think? What does your heart feel? What does your gut know? Often, they tell different truths; let them speak together.
- **In Inner Work**: Practice somatic completion. If anxiety arises, let the body express what it couldn't before—shaking, stretching, making sounds. The body knows how to heal when given permission.

The Koan

What wisdom lives in flesh?

Winter — The Stillness of Flesh

The Season of Transparency

Winter in the body is the recognition that form is not separate from emptiness. The body you take to be solid is mostly space—atoms vibrating, energy in motion, light condensed into apparent solidity.

When awareness rests in this recognition, the body becomes transparent. Not gone, but luminous—matter revealing itself as consciousness taking temporary shape.

The Triadic Lens

- **The Body of Light**

  From mystical traditions East and West: the physical body is the densest layer of a multidimensional form. Beneath flesh is energy, beneath energy is light, beneath light is awareness itself. The body of light is not metaphor; it is direct perception when awareness refines.

- **Dissolving into Space**

  Letting the boundary between body and world soften until you cannot say where one ends and the other begins. The body is not a container but an opening—space aware of itself.

- **The Diamond Body / Rainbow Body**

  In Tibetan Buddhism, masters who complete the practice dissolve the physical body into light at death. The Rainbow Body is the ultimate expression of matter returning to its source while awareness remains. You need not wait for death—practice this transparency now.

Experiencing the Lens

Sit comfortably and close your eyes. Bring awareness to the sensations of the body—warmth, pressure, tingling, pulse.

Now notice the space around sensations. Between breaths, there is a pause. Between heartbeats, stillness. The body is not a solid mass but a rhythm—contraction and release, appearance and disappearance.

Let attention rest in the space rather than the form. Feel how the body emerges from and dissolves back into openness. Hands are not things but awareness condensing into the appearance of hands. Legs not objects, but presence taking shape.

As you sit, imagine your skin's boundary becoming porous. The air outside is the same substance as the air inside your lungs. The space of the room and the space within your body are continuous. Where, exactly, does "you" end and "world" begin?

Let the distinction dissolve. You are not a body in space—you are space temporarily organizing itself as the body.

Rest here. The body remains—sensations still arise—but they no longer feel solid. Everything is vibration, energy, light appearing as form. This is the body of light: matter known as consciousness.

Applications

- **In Daily Life**: When you feel dense or heavy, remember: this body is mostly emptiness. Breathe into that spaciousness. Let awareness dissolve the sense of solidity.
- **In Relationship**: See others not as solid forms but as light temporarily condensed. The same awareness looking out of your eyes looks out of theirs. Different forms, one light.
- **In Inner Work**: At the end of meditation, rest in formless awareness. Let the sense of having a body dissolve. What remains? Not nothing—luminous presence, aware of itself, needing no shape to be.

The Koan

What dissolves when the body turns to light?

Closing Reflection on Domain Four

The body is the ground of all awakening—not because consciousness is material, but because matter is conscious. Every atom of your flesh is awareness taking form, learning itself through touch, taste, movement, breath.

Through these lenses, you have discovered:

- How to inhabit rather than observe the body (Spring)
- How sensation is direct knowing, consciousness meeting itself (Summer)
- How the body is organized intelligence, coherent, and whole (Autumn)
- How form dissolves into light, solidity into space (Winter)

This is embodied spirituality—not escape from the flesh but intimacy with it, not transcendence of matter, but transparency through it.

As you move into Domain Five, the body becomes relational. You will discover that every encounter is touch—consciousness meeting consciousness, form recognizing form, the same awareness greeting itself through infinite faces.

Domain Five

Relationship & Belonging

The Mirror of the Heart

Every face you meet is your face looking back. Every voice you hear is consciousness speaking to itself. Relationship is not two separate beings reaching across distance—it is one awareness recognizing itself through apparent separation.

Yet the illusion of separation is necessary. Without it, there would be no dialogue, no intimacy, no love. The paradox of relationship is that you must be someone to truly meet another, and you must see through that someone to touch what lies beneath.

This domain explores the field between self and other—the invisible space where isolation ends and communion begins. Here, you discover that belonging is not found through conformity, but through transparency: becoming so clear that the light passes through you unobstructed, meeting the light in another without a barrier.

When relationship is seen as spiritual practice, every encounter becomes an opportunity for awakening. The Beloved is not separate from the path—the Beloved *is* the path, mirroring back what remains unseen, calling forth what has not yet emerged.

Spring — The Opening of Connection

The Season of Reaching

Spring in relationship is the first movement toward another—the impulse to be seen, held, understood. This is primal: the infant's cry, the lover's glance, the friend's recognition. Without connection, we cannot become fully human.

Attachment theory holds that our earliest relationships shape how we seek love throughout life. Some learned to trust; others to defend. But the pattern formed in childhood is not destiny—it is the starting point of embodiment. Awareness can repattern how we connect.

The Triadic Lens

- **Secure Base**

  From Bowlby and Ainsworth: the foundation of healthy attachment. When you have a secure base—someone or something you can return to for safety—you can explore the world freely. Without it, life becomes either clinging or isolation.

  In spiritual terms, awareness becomes the secure base. You learn to rest in presence rather than depending solely on external connection.

- **Relational Awareness**

  Perceiving relationship as field rather than transaction. Not "I do this, you do that" but "something moves between us." The relationship itself has intelligence; awareness learns to listen to it.

- **The Circle of Security**

  The rhythm of attachment: moving out to explore, returning for reassurance. Applied to consciousness: you venture into separateness to know yourself, return to unity to rest. Both movements are necessary.

Experiencing the Lens

Bring to mind someone you feel safe with—not necessarily someone you're close to, but someone in whose presence you can simply be.

Notice what this feels like in your body. There is likely a softening—shoulders drop, breath deepens, belly releases. Safety is somatic before it's cognitive.

Now, notice: in their presence, you can be more fully yourself. This is the gift of secure attachment—it creates space for authenticity.

Contrast this with a relationship where you feel guarded. Notice the difference in the body: tightness, holding, constriction. The nervous system is signaling: *not safe to be fully here.*

The work is not to force openness where it isn't appropriate, but to recognize the pattern. How do you typically reach for connection? With confidence, knowing you'll be met? Or with hesitation, expecting rejection?

Feel into this without judgment. The pattern formed long ago, when you had fewer resources. Now, awareness is the resource. Even when the external connection feels uncertain, you can return to the secure foundation of presence.

Applications

- **In Daily Life**: Notice how you bid for connection—the small gestures of reaching out. Do you initiate or wait? Pursue or withdraw? Neither is wrong, but consciousness of the pattern creates choice.
- **In Relationship**: When feeling disconnected from someone you care about, name it: "I'm feeling distant right now. Can we reconnect?" This is vulnerability as practice—trusting that naming disconnection creates the possibility of return.
- **In Inner Work**: Develop relationship with presence. Sit quietly and feel awareness as home base—the place you can always return to, regardless of external circumstances. Let it become your refuge.

The Koan

What is the distance between two hearts?

Summer — The Fire of Intimacy

The Season of Recognition

Summer brings the heat of true meeting—when defenses drop, and you see another not as image or projection, but as living presence. This is intimacy: *in-to-me-see*. Not merging, not losing yourself, but transparent enough that light passes through.

Intimacy requires risk. To be seen fully means revealing what you've kept hidden—the tender places, the unfinished parts, the raw truth beneath the persona. Yet this risk is also freedom. When you stop performing, presence appears.

The Triadic Lens

- **Intersubjectivity**

    The space between subjects where meaning emerges through dialogue. You cannot know yourself alone; identity forms through recognition by another. The "I" requires a "Thou."

- **Resonance**

    Attunement to the subtle field that connects beings. When two people resonate, they synchronize—breathing aligns, gestures mirror, understanding flows without explanation. This is not psychology; it is physics. Consciousness is vibrational.

- **Martin Buber's I-Thou**

    Two ways of meeting: I-It (object, use, distance) and I-Thou (presence, mutuality, sacred encounter). Most relationships oscillate between them. Awakening in relationship is learning to sustain I-Thou—to meet the eternal through the particular.

Experiencing the Lens

Sit facing someone willing to practice with you, or do this alone by imagining someone you care for deeply.

Look at them (or hold their image in awareness) without words. Let your gaze be soft and receptive. You are not analyzing or judging—you are simply present with another presence.

Notice the impulse to look away, to break the intensity. Stay a little longer. The discomfort is not danger; it is unfamiliarity with being truly seen.

Now shift your attention from their appearance to their being. Who is looking out through those eyes? Not the story, the history, the role—who is the awareness meeting yours right now?

In that recognition, something dissolves. The boundary between self and other becomes permeable. You are still distinct, but no longer separate—two waves, one ocean.

If you're doing this with someone present, take turns speaking from this place. Not about thoughts or plans, but from the immediacy of feeling: "Right now I feel..." Let the words be simple, honest. This is intimacy—speaking from presence rather than persona.

Applications

- **In Daily Life**: Practice seeing one person fully each day. Not just noticing them, but truly meeting them—the clerk at the store, the colleague in passing. Let your eyes carry the message: *I see you.*
- **In Relationship**: Create moments of undistracted presence. No devices, no agenda. Sit together, breathe together, feel the field between you. Intimacy is built not through grand gestures but through sustained attention.
- **In Inner Work**: Notice when you objectify others—turning them into functions, roles, problems to solve. This is I-It consciousness. Practice the shift to I-Thou: remembering that every person is a universe, aware and alive.

The Koan

Who meets who in the space between?

Autumn — The Mirror of Projection

The Season of Shadow

Autumn reveals the hard truth: much of what you see in others is yourself, cast outward and forgotten. The irritation you feel, the attraction, the judgment—each is a mirror reflecting what remains unconscious within.

This is not to dismiss the reality of others, but to recognize that relationship is where the psyche completes itself. What you cannot own in yourself, you project onto another. And there it waits, asking to be retrieved.

The Triadic Lens

- **Projection**

  Seeing in others what you deny in yourself. The disowned anger appears as someone else's hostility. The unlived creativity appears as envy of another's gifts. Every strong reaction is an invitation to look inward.

- **Shadow Work**

  Reclaiming the disowned. Not to excuse others' behavior, but to recognize your participation in the relational field. When you withdraw projection, both you and the relationship clarify.

- **The Imago Dialogue**

  From Harville Hendrix: structured practice for conscious relationship. You mirror what you hear without interpretation, validate the other's reality, and empathize with their experience. This dissolves projection by honoring difference.

Experiencing the Lens

Think of someone who consistently irritates you. Notice what specifically bothers you—are they too controlling? Too careless? Too loud?

Now ask: *Where in myself does this quality exist, denied or suppressed?*

This is difficult. The mind will resist: "I'm not like that at all!" But stay with it. You don't have to express the quality the way they do. Perhaps they're overtly controlling while you control through withdrawal. Perhaps they're recklessly spontaneous, while you're rigidly planned.

The shadow is not always opposite to your persona—it's what you've rejected to maintain your self-image.

When you find the thread, feel into it. What would it be like to own this quality consciously? Not to become what you've rejected, but to integrate its energy without defense?

Now practice the Imago Dialogue in your mind, or with someone willing:

- **Mirror**: Repeat back what you heard without adding interpretation. "What I'm hearing is..."
- **Validate**: Acknowledge that from their perspective, their experience makes sense. "I can see how you would feel that way."
- **Empathize**: Imagine what it feels like to be them. "And I imagine that feels..."

This is not agreement. It is recognition that their reality is real *for them*, even if it differs from yours.

Applications

- **In Daily Life**: When someone triggers a strong reaction, pause before responding. Ask: *What in me is being activated?* Often, the intensity points not to them but to your own unfinished business.
- **In Relationship**: Make projection conscious by naming it: "I notice I'm feeling defensive, and I'm wondering if some of what I'm reacting to is mine rather than yours." This humility transforms conflict into inquiry.
- **In Inner Work**: Keep a projection journal. When you notice a strong attraction or aversion to someone, write what you see in them. Then ask: *How does this quality live in me, hidden or distorted?* Let the mirror do its work.

The Koan

What do I see in you that I cannot see in myself?

Winter — The Communion of Being

The Season of Unity

Winter dissolves the last boundary between self and other. Not through merging—you remain distinct—but through recognition: the same awareness looks out of every eye, the same presence breathes every breath.

This is not philosophy but direct experience. When projection clears and intimacy deepens, you begin to feel the truth: love is not something you give or receive—it is what you are, meeting itself in form.

The Triadic Lens

- **Nondual Love**

    Love beyond subject and object, beyond giver and receiver. When you rest in awareness, love is not an emotion you feel toward another—it is the nature of consciousness recognizing itself everywhere.

- **Unity Consciousness**

    Perceiving the field rather than separate beings. Not that individuality disappears, but that it's recognized as temporary localization of one infinite presence.

- **The Beloved in All Forms (Sufi)**

    Every face is the face of the Beloved. Every encounter is God meeting God. When this is seen, reverence replaces judgment, wonder replaces expectation.

Experiencing the Lens

Sit quietly and bring to mind someone you love—not romantically necessarily, but someone whose presence opens your heart.

Feel that love. Where does it live in your body? Notice it's not confined to thought—it's palpable, warm, expansive.

Now notice: the love you feel is not coming from them. It's arising in you, through you. They are the occasion for it, but you are its source.

This is not diminishing them—it's recognizing that love is your nature, not your reaction. The beloved reveals what was always present.

Now expand this recognition. Feel the same love toward someone neutral—a stranger, someone you barely know. The love is still here; it doesn't require special conditions. It is simply the warmth of awareness meeting form.

Finally, feel it toward someone difficult. Not forcing affection, but recognizing: they, too, are awareness in form, trying to find their way. The same life pulses through them as through you.

This is the secret: when you rest as love, every encounter is communion. You are not loving others—you are being love, encountering itself in infinite disguises.

Applications

- **In Daily Life**: Practice seeing the sacred in ordinary encounters. The person in line at the grocery store, the neighbor walking past—each is consciousness, temporary and precious. Let your eyes carry blessing.
- **In Relationship**: When conflict arises, remember: this person is not an enemy or obstacle. They are awareness, just like you, expressing through different conditioning. This doesn't excuse harm, but it places everything in a larger context.
- **In Inner Work**: Meditate on the phrase: *All beings are expressions of the same awareness.* Let it become felt rather than thought. When it lands, separation is revealed as illusion—beautiful, necessary, but ultimately transparent.

The Koan

Where does your heart end and mine begin?

Closing Reflection on Domain Five

Relationship is the crucible where the illusion of separation burns away. Through connection, intimacy, shadow, and union, you discover that you have never been alone—not because someone is always there, but because alone and together are two descriptions of one reality.

Through these lenses, you have learned:

- How to reach for connection while resting in presence (Spring)
- How to meet another as living presence, not projection (Summer)
- How to retrieve what you've cast onto others, reclaiming wholeness (Autumn)
- How to recognize the same awareness in every form (Winter)

As you move into Domain Six, the descent deepens. You will meet what you have most rejected, denied, hidden—the shadow that waits not as enemy but as the dark half of wholeness, asking to be known.

Domain Six

Shadow & Wholeness

The Dark Half of Awakening

Light without shadow is blinding. Goodness without darkness is sterile. Every spiritual path that denies the shadow becomes its unwitting servant.

The shadow is not evil—it is simply what you refused to be. Every quality you rejected to become acceptable, every impulse you suppressed to feel safe, every aspect of humanness you disowned to maintain your self-image. All of it still lives, but underground, where it grows wild and strange.

Most spiritual teachings emphasize light, including transcendence, peace, love, and clarity. But wholeness requires descent. You cannot rise until you've felt the ground beneath you, and the ground includes everything—rage and tenderness, darkness and radiance, the howl and the hymn.

This domain is an invitation into the underworld of your psyche. Not to indulge what you find there, but to reclaim it. When the shadow is brought into consciousness, its energy becomes available. What was once compulsion transforms into choice. What was once wound becomes wisdom.

The path to wholeness does not go around the darkness—it goes through it, with eyes open and heart willing.

Spring — Meeting What Was Cast Away

The Season of Recognition

Spring begins when you notice the gap—the places where your self-image ends and truth begins. You present yourself as patient, but rage simmers beneath the surface. You pride yourself on independence, but a deep longing aches in the night. The person you believe yourself to be is only half the story.

The shadow forms early. As a child, you learned which parts of yourself were acceptable and which had to be hidden. "Don't be so loud." "Stop crying." "Be nice." Each correction carved away a piece of aliveness, and you forgot it was ever yours.

But nothing truly disappears. What is denied goes underground, where it continues to live—not as an integrated aspect but as an autonomous force, erupting in moments of projection, compulsion, or inexplicable reaction.

The Triadic Lens

- **The Personal Shadow (Jung)**

    Everything you decided you are not. If your persona is "I am kind," your shadow holds "I am cruel." If your identity is "I am strong," your shadow carries "I am weak." The shadow is not the opposite of who you are—it is the rejected half of wholeness.

- **Compassionate Inquiry**

    Approaching the shadow not with judgment but with curiosity. Not "Why am I like this?" but "What is this part trying to protect?" Every defense once served survival; it can be honored even as it's outgrown.

- **The 3-2-1 Shadow Process (Integral)**

    A three-step practice for reclaiming projection:

    - **3rd Person**: Name what you see in another ("He is arrogant")
    - **2nd Person**: Speak to it as "you" ("You are arrogant, and you...")
    - **1st Person**: Own it as "I" ("I am arrogant when...")

    The shift from 3rd to 1st person is alchemical—what was outside becomes inside, and energy returns.

Experiencing the Lens

Think of someone you strongly dislike—not someone who harmed you, but someone whose mere presence irritates you. What quality do they embody that you find intolerable? Arrogance? Neediness? Recklessness?

Write it down: "They are [quality]."

Now shift to second person. Speak to this quality as if addressing the person: "You are [quality]. You make me feel... You remind me of..."

Notice what arises. Often there's heat, charge, emotion. This is the shadow activating.

Now comes the difficult part. Shift to first person: "I am [quality]."

Feel the resistance. The mind will protest: "No, I'm not like that at all!" But stay with it. You don't express this quality the way they do, but it lives in you somewhere.

Perhaps if they're overtly arrogant, you're covertly superior—judging rather than boasting. Perhaps if they're openly needy, you're secretly desperate but hide it. The shadow is not identical to what you project; it's the same energy in a different form.

When you can say "I am this" without shame or defense, the projection dissolves. The energy that was locked in judgment becomes available for integration.

Applications

- **In Daily Life**: Notice what consistently annoys you in others. Each irritation is a teacher pointing toward disowned parts of yourself. Make a list: "I can't stand people who are..." Then ask: "Where does this quality live in me?"
- **In Relationship**: When you find yourself judging someone harshly, pause. The intensity is the clue. Strong reactions indicate shadow. Practice the 3-2-1 process: name it, speak to it, own it.
- **In Inner Work**: Create a shadow journal. Each time you notice a strong projection—positive or negative—write it down and work it through the three positions. Over time, you'll recognize patterns. These are the places calling for integration.

The Koan

What part of me am I refusing to see?

Summer — The Fire of Integration

The Season of Reclamation

Summer brings active engagement with the shadow. Not just recognizing what you've denied, but welcoming it back. This is the most challenging work—not because the shadow is dangerous, but because the ego built its identity on *not* being this.

To integrate shadow means loosening the self-concept you've defended for years. "I'm a good person" must expand to include moments of pettiness. "I'm gentle" must make space for the times you want to destroy something. The persona's need for consistency collides with truth's demand for wholeness.

Yet there is also the golden shadow—the rejected gifts, the unlived potential, the brilliance you decided was too much. Reclaiming this requires even more courage than owning darkness. To be fully yourself is to risk being seen.

The Triadic Lens

- **The Golden Shadow**

  The positive qualities you've disowned—strength, beauty, power, wisdom. You see them in others and feel envy or awe, never recognizing they're yours. The golden shadow is often larger than the dark one.

- **Both/And Consciousness**

  Holding paradox. You are kind *and* cruel, strong *and* fragile, generous *and* selfish. Not sequentially, but simultaneously. Wholeness is not being one thing; it's being capacious enough to hold all things.

- **Active Imagination (Jung)**

  Dialoguing with the shadow as if it were a separate being. You sit, invoke an aspect you've denied, and let it speak. Not fantasy—phenomenological encounter. The shadow has intelligence; when given voice, it reveals what it guards.

Experiencing the Lens

Sit quietly and call to mind an aspect of yourself you've kept hidden—perhaps anger, sexuality, ambition, neediness, arrogance. Something you've judged as "bad" or "unspiritual."

Imagine this aspect as a figure sitting across from you. Give it form: what does it look like? How does it move? What's its energy?

Now invite it to speak. Ask: "Why are you here? What do you want? What are you protecting?"

Listen without editing. Let words, images, or sensations arise. Often the shadow reveals that it's been trying to help—the rage protecting boundaries, the neediness seeking connection, the arrogance defending worthiness.

When you understand its purpose, the relationship shifts. The shadow is not enemy but ally. It holds energy you exiled because you didn't know how to integrate it.

Now do the same with the golden shadow. What quality do you admire in others—brilliance, confidence, creativity, power? Imagine this quality as a figure and ask: "Why have I rejected you? What would it cost to embody you?"

Often, the golden shadow was rejected because it felt unsafe. To be brilliant might invite envy. To be powerful might isolate you. To be beautiful might attract unwanted attention. The child made a wise choice then. The adult can make a different one now.

Applications

- **In Daily Life**: When you notice envy—someone has something you want—pause. Envy is the golden shadow announcing itself. Instead of dismissing it, ask: "What quality are they expressing that wants to live through me?"
- **In Relationship**: Share something you've kept hidden—not to dump or confess, but to practice wholeness. "I notice I feel competitive with you sometimes." "I want attention more than I let on." This vulnerability is integration happening aloud.
- **In Inner Work**: Practice active imagination regularly. Pick one shadow aspect and engage in dialogue with it weekly. Over time, it stops feeling foreign and begins to feel like a lost part of yourself coming home.

The Koan

What brilliance am I afraid to claim?

Autumn — The Collective Shadow

The Season of Deepening

Autumn reveals that shadow is not only personal—it is collective. The qualities you reject are often the ones your culture, family, or tribe has deemed unacceptable. You carry not just your disowned parts but the disowned parts of your lineage.

This is where shadow work becomes intertwined with politics, culture, and archetypes. The shadow includes what your gender is not supposed to express, what your race is not allowed to feel, and what your religion has condemned. To integrate the collective shadow is to refuse inherited shame.

The Triadic Lens

- **The Cultural Shadow**

    Every society creates an idealized self-image and casts away what contradicts it. In America, the shadow includes vulnerability, dependence, and failure. In other cultures, different aspects are rejected. You inherit these rejections without choosing them.

- **Archetypal Awareness**

    Recognizing that beneath personal patterns are universal ones. The shadow you carry is also Kali, Dionysus, the Trickster, the Destroyer. When you meet it as an archetype rather than a personal failing, its power and purpose become visible.

- **Scapegoating (René Girard)**

    Groups maintain cohesion by projecting their collective shadow onto an outsider—the scapegoat who carries what the group refuses to acknowledge. When you recognize this mechanism, you stop participating in it.

Experiencing the Lens

Reflect on the values you inherited—from family, culture, and religion. What were you taught was good? What was condemned?

Now ask: what did that teaching force you to reject? If you were taught "success above all," you may have exiled your need for rest. If you learned "be nice, don't make waves," you may have buried your anger.

Feel into this collective inheritance. These are not just your shadows—they belong to the field you were born into. And yet they live through you, shaping how you perceive and what you allow yourself to be.

Now consider the collective shadows of your culture. What does your society idealize, and what does it demonize? In the U.S., independence is elevated; dependence is weakness. Productivity is valued; rest is laziness. Strength is praised, while vulnerability is often seen as a failure.

Notice how these cultural beliefs have shaped your own shadow. The parts of yourself you reject are often the parts your culture has already rejected.

The work is not to rebel against your culture but to see through its projections. When you reclaim what has been collectively disowned, you participate in cultural healing—not by trying to change others, but by becoming whole yourself.

Applications

- **In Daily Life**: When you notice yourself judging a group—political, cultural, religious—pause. What quality do they embody that your group has rejected? The judgment is often collective shadow made visible.
- **In Relationship**: Notice how you carry roles inherited from family or culture. If you're a woman taught to be accommodating, where is your refusal? If you're a man taught to be strong, where is your tenderness? Reclaiming these is both personal and collective work.
- **In Inner Work**: Study mythology. The gods and monsters are not metaphors—they are the collective psyche's shadow and light made visible. When you recognize yourself in Medusa, Prometheus, or Persephone, you're touching the archetypal dimension of your own experience.

The Koan

Whose shadow am I carrying?

Winter — The Luminous Dark

The Season of Union

Winter dissolves the distinction between light and shadow, not by erasing difference, but by revealing that both arise from the same source. Darkness is not the opposite of light—it is light hidden, coiled, waiting.

This is the mystical dimension of shadow work: the recognition that what you call darkness is often the depth you haven't yet learned to see. The soul's night is not absence of God but intimacy with God beyond all images.

When you stop dividing reality into good and bad, acceptable and unacceptable, the war within ceases. What remains is wholeness—vast enough to include everything, tender enough to reject nothing.

The Triadic Lens

- **Coincidentia Oppositorum**

    Nicholas of Cusa's term: the unity of opposites. At the highest level of consciousness, contradictions merge. Light and dark, good and evil, sacred and profane—all are movements of the One expressing itself.

- **Nondual Embrace**

    Holding all experience—light and shadow, beauty and horror—as belonging to the wholeness of being. Not moral relativism, but recognition that consciousness includes everything without being defined by anything.

- **The Dark Night of the Soul (St. John of the Cross)**

    The spiritual crisis where all consolation is stripped away and the soul meets God in darkness. This is not punishment but purification—the ego's images of the divine dissolving so the divine itself can be known.

Experiencing the Lens

Sit in darkness—literal darkness, if possible. Let your eyes adjust. Notice how the dark is not empty—it is full of presence, subtle gradations, alive.

Now bring to mind something you've judged as your darkest aspect—shame, rage, despair, the part you least want anyone to see.

Instead of turning away, move toward it. Feel where it lives in your body. Let it be here fully, without story or defense.

As you stay present with this darkness, something begins to shift. The darkness is not evil—it is energy without outlet, love turned inward, power without permission to express.

Ask it: *What do you carry for me? What are you protecting?*

Often the darkest shadow holds the deepest care. The rage protects something precious. The shame guards innocence. The despair mourns what matters most.

When you meet the shadow with this recognition, it transforms—not into light, but into luminous darkness. It remains what it is, but its purpose becomes clear. It is not here to destroy you but to complete you.

Now rest in the recognition that light and shadow are not two. Every saint has shadow; every sinner, light. The division is conceptual. Reality is whole.

Applications

- **In Daily Life**: When you encounter something you judge as "bad"—in yourself or another—pause. Ask: "What if this too belongs? What if this darkness serves wholeness in a way I cannot yet see?"
- **In Relationship**: Practice loving what you once condemned. Not condoning harm, but recognizing that even the most destructive impulse began as an attempt at protection or expression. When you see this, compassion becomes possible.
- **In Inner Work**: Sit with paradox. You are selfish and generous. Wise and foolish. Awake and asleep. Let these opposites rest together without resolution. Wholeness is not one-sided; it is all-sided.

The Koan

What shines in the darkness that cannot see?

Closing Reflection on Domain Six

The shadow is not obstacle to awakening—it is awakening's completion. Every quality you rejected is energy waiting to be integrated. Every darkness you denied is depth asking to be known.

Through these lenses, you have learned:

- How to recognize what you've cast away and begin reclaiming it (Spring)
- How to integrate both dark and golden shadow, becoming whole (Summer)
- How shadow is collective as well as personal, inherited, and archetypal (Autumn)
- How darkness and light are one reality, seen through different eyes (Winter)

This work is never finished. New layers of shadow emerge as consciousness expands. But once you've tasted wholeness—the relief of no longer defending an image, the freedom of being fully human—you will not want to return to the exhausting performance of perfection.

As you move into Domain Seven, the mind itself becomes transparent. You will discover that thought, like shadow, is not the enemy. When awareness sees through thinking, the mind becomes servant rather than master, and wisdom flows unobstructed.

Domain Seven

The Mind's Mirror

Thought and the Space That Holds It

The mind is not your enemy. It is a brilliant instrument—organizing chaos into meaning, translating the infinite into the navigable, weaving memory and imagination into the story called "my life."

But the mind becomes tyrannical when you forget you are not it. When awareness is identified with thought, thinking becomes compulsive. The inner voice never stops, and you mistake its commentary for truth.

This domain explores the relationship between awareness and thinking. You will learn to see thought as phenomenon rather than identity, to rest in the gaps between mental activity, and to discover that the mind—when transparent to awareness—becomes not an obstacle but an oracle.

The work is simple but not easy: learning to be *with* thought rather than *as* thought. When this shift occurs, thinking continues but loses its grip. The mind becomes a mirror—reflecting reality without distorting it, serving presence rather than obscuring it.

Spring — The Awakening of Thought

The Season of Separation

Spring begins when you notice: *I am not my thoughts*. This seems obvious intellectually, but it is revolutionary experientially. Most people spend entire lifetimes identified with the stream of mental commentary, never realizing they are the awareness in which that stream flows.

The Triadic Lens

- **Metacognition**

  Thinking about thinking. The moment you observe a thought, you've stepped outside identification. The observed thought cannot be the observer. This creates distance—not separation that isolates, but space that liberates.

- **Witnessing Awareness**

  The ability to observe mental activity without being caught up in it. Not suppressing thought, not following it—simply seeing it arise, move, and dissolve like clouds across the sky.

- **Vipassana (Insight Meditation)**

  The practice of noting: *thinking, planning, remembering, judging*. Each label interrupts identification and returns awareness to its natural position as witness.

Experiencing the Lens

Sit quietly and watch the mind. Do not try to control it—let thoughts come freely. Your only task is to notice them.

When a thought appears—*I should do this, I forgot that, what if this happens*—silently note it: *thinking*. Not as judgment but as recognition. Thought is happening; you are aware of it happening.

Notice the gap between awareness and thought. There is you, watching. There is thought, appearing in the space of awareness. They are not the same.

This is not a special state. It is the natural structure of consciousness—you have always been the one watching thought. You simply forgot, collapsing watcher and watched into false unity.

Practice for ten minutes. Each time you notice you've been lost in thought, smile. That noticing is awakening—awareness recognizing itself again.

Applications

- **In Daily Life**: Label thoughts as they arise. *Planning. Worrying. Remembering.* This simple act creates space and dissolves the illusion that you *are* the thought.

- **In Relationship**: When someone says something that triggers a strong reaction, notice: *defensive thought, judgmental thought.* The thought is visitor, not truth. You can choose whether to speak from it or let it pass.
- **In Inner Work**: End each meditation by reflecting: *Who was aware of the thoughts?* The answer is never found in thinking—it is the silence that remains when thinking stops.

The Koan

Who watches the thought?

Summer — The Fire of Mind

The Season of Energy

Summer reveals thought not as static content but as energy in motion. The mind is not a thing, but a process—electricity moving through neural networks, patterns firing and dissolving, awareness taking temporary shape as a concept, image, or memory.

When you see thought as energy, you begin to feel its texture. Some thoughts are heavy, dense, repetitive. Others are light, swift, dissolving the moment they arise. The quality of mental energy reflects the state of consciousness.

The Triadic Lens

- **Thought as a Form of Energy**

    Every thought carries an energetic signature. Anxious thoughts create contraction; creative thoughts expand awareness. Judgmental thoughts drain; curious thoughts enliven.

- **Flow States**

    When mind and awareness align, thinking becomes effortless. No resistance, no self-consciousness—just consciousness moving as thought, thought dissolving back into consciousness.

- **The Hermetic Principle of Mentalism**

    "The All is Mind." Consciousness is primary; thought is its expression. When this is seen, you stop treating thoughts as invasions and recognize them as movements of your own awareness.

Experiencing the Lens

Sit and bring attention to the energetic quality of thinking. Not what you're thinking, but how thought feels.

Notice: some thoughts arrive with heaviness—worry, resentment, regret. Feel the density in your chest, the contraction in your belly. These thoughts carry stagnant energy.

Other thoughts arrive lightly—curiosity, inspiration, gratitude. Feel the openness in your chest, the lift in your posture. These thoughts carry flowing energy.

You cannot control what thoughts arise, but you can notice which ones you feed. When heavy thought appears, you can observe it without lending it energy. When light thought appears, you can allow it space to unfold.

Now experiment with shifting the energy. If anxious thoughts dominate, do not fight them. Instead, invite a different quality: *What am I curious about right now? What feels alive?* Watch how the mental atmosphere shifts not through suppression but through redirection.

Applications

- **In Daily Life**: Notice the energetic cost of rumination. When the mind loops—replaying conversations, rehearsing arguments—feel the drain. Then, consciously shift: take three deep breaths, ask a generative question, and redirect your attention to sensation.
- **In Relationship**: Before difficult conversations, check the quality of your thoughts. Are they accusatory? Defensive? Rigid? Shift the energy first—breathe, soften, open to curiosity—then speak. The conversation will follow the energy you bring.
- **In Inner Work**: Practice entering flow. Choose an activity—such as writing, walking, or creating—and give it your full attention. Notice when self-consciousness arises (*Am I doing this right?*) and gently return to the doing itself. Thought becomes servant, awareness remains master.

The Koan

What moves when the mind is still?

Autumn — The Space Between

The Season of Silence

Autumn reveals what Spring and Summer prepared you for: the gaps. Between thoughts, there is space. Between breaths, pause. Between sounds, silence. The mind is not continuous—it is punctuated by moments of no-mind, brief glimpses of awareness resting as simplicity itself.

Most people rush past these gaps, filling every pause with more thinking. But the gap is not empty—it is full. Full of presence, full of clarity, full of the awareness that holds all thought.

The Triadic Lens

- **The Gap in Consciousness**

    The interval between the end of one thought and the beginning of the next. It lasts less than a second, yet it contains infinity. In that gap, awareness knows itself directly.

- **Resting Attention**

    Not concentrating on the gap—that would be another form of effort. Simply noticing when thought ceases, and being there, in the silence, before the next thought begins.

- **Zen Shikantaza (Just Sitting)**

    The practice of presence without object. Not meditating *on* something, but simply being awareness, aware. Thought comes and goes; the sitting remains.

Experiencing the Lens

Sit and watch the mind. Instead of noting the thoughts, notice the spaces between them.

After a thought completes—*I need to email her*—there is a moment before the next thought begins. Rest there. Just for an instant, you are thought-free. Aware, alive, but not thinking.

The gap may be brief—half a second, less. It doesn't matter. What matters is recognizing it. In that recognition, awareness touches itself.

As you continue, the gaps may lengthen. Not because you're suppressing thought, but because awareness resting in itself is more satisfying than the endless stream of commentary. The mind begins to quiet naturally.

This is the secret: you do not need to stop thinking. You only need to recognize the space in which thoughts arise. That space is always here, always silent, always still—even when filled with mental noise.

Applications

- **In Daily Life**: Between activities, pause. Do not immediately fill the space with a phone, a task, or a thought. Let there be a moment of nothing—just presence, breathing, being.
- **In Relationship**: In conversation, notice the silence between words. Most people are already preparing their response while the other is speaking. Practice resting in the gap—truly receiving what was said before formulating what to say next.
- **In Inner Work**: Let meditation become simpler. No technique, no goal. Just sitting, being. When thought arises, let it pass. When silence appears, rest there. The work is not creating silence, but rather recognizing the silence that is already present.

The Koan

What speaks in the silence?

_____

_____

_____

Winter — The Mirror of Mind

The Season of Transparency

Winter dissolves the final boundary: the distinction between mind and awareness. You discover that thinking is not separate from consciousness—it is consciousness expressing itself, awareness taking temporary form.

When this is seen, the mind becomes transparent. Thought continues, but it no longer obscures. It is like writing on water—visible for a moment, dissolving immediately, leaving the water unchanged.

The Triadic Lens

- **Non-Conceptual Knowing**

    Direct awareness prior to thought. You know you exist before you think "I exist." You perceive the world before you name what you see. This knowing is immediate, unmediated, always present.

- **Direct Recognition**

    Not arriving at understanding through reasoning, but recognizing what is already obvious. The mirror does not need to understand reflection—it simply reflects.

- **The Zen Koan**

    Questions designed to exhaust conceptual mind: *What is your original face before you were born? What is the sound of one hand clapping?* The koan is not solved; it dissolves the solver.

Experiencing the Lens

Sit in silence and ask: *What am I before thought arises?*

Do not answer with thinking. Let the question settle into the body, into the space of awareness.

When thought tries to answer—*I am consciousness, I am awareness, I am presence*—notice that these are still thoughts *about* what you are, not the direct recognition itself.

Go deeper. What is here before any concept, before any name, before the first "I"?

This cannot be grasped by mind. It can only be recognized—the way you recognize your face in a mirror without needing to think *that's me*.

You are this. Not the thoughts about this, but this—the aware presence reading these words, the silence holding the sound of your breath, the openness in which world appears.

Rest here. Thoughts will come—let them. They are not other than this awareness. They are this awareness, temporarily taking form as thought, then dissolving back into silence.

The mirror remains clear whether images appear in it or not.

Applications

- **In Daily Life**: Throughout the day, pause and recognize: *I am aware*. Not "I am aware *of* this" but simply the bare fact of being conscious. This recognition is awakening.
- **In Relationship**: When someone speaks, listen not just to their words but to the awareness in them that is speaking. The same consciousness in you is in them. Two mirrors reflecting the same light.
- **In Inner Work**: Let koans live in you. Carry one question—*Who am I?* or *What is this?*—not to answer it but to let it dissolve the answerer. When the mind surrenders, recognition dawns.

The Koan

What remains when thought stops?

Closing Reflection on Domain Seven

The mind is not the problem—identification with mind is. When awareness recognizes itself as the space in which thought occurs, the war between silence and thinking ends. Both belong. Both are expressions of consciousness knowing itself.

Through these lenses, you discovered:

- How to witness thought rather than be thought (Spring)
- How mental energy moves and can be redirected (Summer)
- How silence lives in the gaps between thinking (Autumn)
- How awareness and mind are not two (Winter)

The mind, when transparent, becomes what it always was: a mirror reflecting reality without distortion, a servant of presence rather than its master.

As you move into Domain Eight, the question deepens: not *what* you think but *why* you seek meaning at all. The search for purpose reveals itself as the soul's longing to know why it is here—and the gradual discovery that being here is the answer.

Domain Eight

Meaning & Purpose

The Question That Dissolves Itself

Why am I here?

Every human asks this eventually. Not as philosophy but as hunger—the soul wanting to know if its existence matters, if there is reason beneath the chaos, if this brief flicker of consciousness serves something larger than survival.

The search for meaning is sacred. It lifts awareness from the mechanical into the meaningful, from mere being into purposeful becoming. Yet the search itself can become obstacle. When you believe meaning must be found, discovered, earned, you overlook what is already here: the simple fact that you are alive, aware, participating in mystery.

This domain explores how the search for meaning matures. Early, it seeks answers: *What should I do? What is my calling?* Later, it seeks alignment: *How do I serve? What wants to live through me?* Finally, it dissolves into recognition: *Being here is itself the meaning. Presence is the purpose.*

This is not resignation. It is the end of seeking and the beginning of seeing—the shift from meaning as destination to meaning as the texture of awakened life.

Spring — The Seed of Wonder

The Season of Question

Spring begins with genuine not-knowing. Not confusion but innocence—the willingness to live the question without rushing toward answer.

Most meaning-seeking is anxiety disguised as inquiry: *If I find my purpose, I'll finally feel okay.* But true wonder has no agenda. It asks because asking itself is aliveness.

The Triadic Lens

- **Existential Curiosity**

  The impulse to wonder about being itself. Not *What should I do with my life?* but *What is it to be alive?* This shift transforms the quest for purpose from problem-solving into contemplation.

- **Appreciative Inquiry**

  Focusing not on what's missing but on what's already meaningful. Instead of asking "What's wrong with my life?" ask "What gives my life vitality?" Meaning is uncovered, not invented.

- **Logotherapy (Viktor Frankl)**

  Meaning can always be found—in work, in love, in suffering. Even when circumstances are unbearable, the freedom to choose how you meet them remains. Purpose is not what happens to you but how you respond to what happens.

Experiencing the Lens

Sit with the question: *What gives my life meaning right now?*

Not what *should* give it meaning, or what you wish gave it meaning, but what actually does. Notice what arises—perhaps relationships, creative work, the beauty of morning light, the simple fact of being present.

Let these recognitions land in the body. Meaning is not abstract; it registers as warmth, opening, aliveness.

Now ask: *What would I do if I knew my life had meaning simply because I'm alive?*

Feel how this shifts the inquiry. You're not seeking purpose to justify existence—you're exploring how existence already expresses through your particular form.

Applications

- **In Daily Life**: Notice moments when life feels meaningful without effort—watching a child laugh, tending a garden, listening to music. These are not distractions from purpose; they are purpose revealing itself.
- **In Relationship**: Ask loved ones what gives their lives meaning. Listen not to compare but to witness how meaning is plural, personal, constantly unfolding.

- **In Inner Work:** Journal without agenda. Begin with "What matters to me is..." and let the pen move. Meaning speaks when the mind stops demanding answers.

The Koan

What if meaning is not found but felt?

_____
_____
_____
_____
_____
_____
_____
_____
_____
_____
_____
_____

Summer — The Fire of Direction

The Season of Alignment

Summer brings clarity: meaning becomes movement. You sense what calls you forward—not as an obligation, but as a resonance. The question shifts from "Why am I here?" to "What wants to happen through me?"

This is not the ego deciding its purpose, but awareness recognizing the current already moving through life.

The Triadic Lens

- Teleology

  The recognition that everything moves toward its fulfillment—the acorn toward the oak, the infant toward maturity, the soul toward its unique expression. Purpose is not imposed; it unfolds.

- Intuitive Knowing

  Guidance that arises not from thinking but from deeper intelligence—the body's yes, the heart's resonance, the subtle sense of rightness. Intuition does not explain; it recognizes.

- Ikigai (Japanese)

  The intersection of four questions:

    - What do you love?
    - What are you good at?
    - What does the world need?
    - What can you be sustained by?

  Where these meet, purpose becomes embodied.

Experiencing the Lens

Ask yourself: *What am I drawn toward that I keep dismissing as impractical?*

Often purpose whispers before it shouts. The quiet longing, the recurring image, the thing you do "just for fun" that lights you up—these are clues.

Now, feel into the four questions of Ikigai. Not to force an answer but to sense where resonance lives.

1. What do you love? Not what you think you should love, but what actually brings aliveness.
2. What are you good at? Not just skills but qualities—presence, listening, seeing patterns, holding space.
3. What does the world need? Feel into this broadly—not saving humanity, but where does your particular form of care want to flow?
4. What sustains you? Not just money but energy, meaning, connection.

Let these questions live in you. Purpose does not arrive fully formed; it reveals itself through attention.

Applications

- **In Daily Life**: Follow small yeses. When something calls—a conversation, a project, a walk in the woods—say yes without needing to know why. Purpose emerges through participation, not planning.
- **In Relationship**: Notice who draws out your aliveness. Purpose often reveals itself through connection—not codependence, but mutual flourishing.
- **In Inner Work**: Trust the body's guidance. When considering a choice, feel into it: does your chest open or contract? Purpose speaks somatically before it speaks conceptually.

The Koan

What does life want from me?

Autumn — The Revision of Story

The Season of Surrender

Autumn reveals the hard truth: meaning is not fixed. What once felt like purpose can complete itself, leaving you in a void. The calling that sustained you for years may dissolve, and no new calling appears to take its place.

This is not failure—it is transformation. The old meaning must die for new meaning to be born.

The Triadic Lens

- **Existential Crisis as Initiation**

  The loss of meaning is not pathology but passage. Every authentic life includes moments when the familiar falls away and nothing arises to replace it. This void is not empty—it is fertile.

- **Narrative Flexibility**

  Holding your story lightly enough that it can change. You were this; now you're becoming something else. The self is not fixed; purpose is not permanent.

- **The Hero's Journey (Revisited)**

  The cycle of call, descent, and return. But now you see: the return is not to the same place. You come back changed, and what once mattered may no longer matter. This is growth.

Experiencing the Lens

Reflect on a time when meaning collapsed—a loss, a transition, a moment when what sustained you no longer did.

Feel into that void without trying to fill it. What was it like to not know?

Often, the void is terrifying because the ego equates meaning with survival. But awareness does not need meaning to exist; it simply is.

Now ask: *What emerged after the void?* Not immediately, but eventually. Often, a new orientation, a deeper truth, a purpose that could only be born through the death of the old.

This is the rhythm of meaning: appearance, dissolution, renewal. Each cycle deepens.

Applications

- **In Daily Life**: When purpose feels absent, resist the reflex to fill the void immediately. Let there be not-knowing. The space is itself purposeful—it's gestation.
- **In Relationship**: When connection feels stale, don't abandon it—explore what's completing and what's wanting to be born. Meaning in relationship also cycles.
- **In Inner Work**: Sit with meaninglessness. Not as defeat but as openness. The ego craves purpose; awareness rests as it is. Let the difference become clear.

The Koan

What remains when purpose falls away?

Winter — The Stillness of Being

The Season of Completion

Winter dissolves the search. Not because meaning is found but because the distinction between seeker and meaning collapses. You are not here to fulfill a purpose—you are the purpose, expressing itself.

This is the end of striving and the beginning of simple presence. Life continues, action continues, but there is no one trying to make life meaningful. Meaning is the texture of awareness meeting each moment without demand.

The Triadic Lens

- **Being as Meaning**

    The recognition that existence itself is sufficient. You do not need to justify being alive. The fact of awareness is already complete, already whole.

- **Contemplative Presence**

    Resting as what is, prior to all interpretation. Not seeking meaning but being the field in which meaning arises and dissolves.

- **The Tao Te Ching**

    "The Tao does nothing, yet nothing is left undone." When you align with the flow of being, action arises effortlessly. Purpose is not imposed; it is expressed through surrender to what is.

Experiencing the Lens

Sit and let go of all questions about meaning. Just be here.

Breath moving in and out. Heart beating. Awareness aware. No reason needed. No purpose required.

Feel how the mind resists this. It wants to *do* something, to figure something out, to ensure that this moment matters.

Let the resistance be there. Beneath it, notice the simple fact: you are here. Alive. Aware.

This is not nothing. This is everything.

When the search for meaning ends, meaning is everywhere. The warmth of tea, the sound of rain, the presence of another, the breath itself—each is complete, requiring no justification.

Applications

In Daily Life: Stop asking if what you're doing is meaningful enough. Do it fully. Wash the dish as if it matters—because in this moment, it does. Meaning is presence, not evaluation.

In Relationship: Be with others without needing the interaction to mean something. Just presence meeting presence. This is the deepest purpose.

In Inner Work: Let practice become purposeless. Not sitting to become enlightened, but sitting because sitting is what's happening. When effort ends, grace begins.

The Koan

What is here before purpose is sought?

Closing Reflection on Domain Eight

The search for meaning is the soul's homesickness for its own presence. You seek purpose because you've forgotten that being alive is already purposeful—not because it serves something else, but because aliveness is its own justification.

Through these lenses, you discovered:

- How wonder opens the question of meaning without demanding answer (Spring)
- How purpose emerges through alignment with what calls you (Summer)
- How meaning dissolves and reforms, cycling through death and rebirth (Autumn)
- How being itself is the meaning you've been seeking (Winter)

The journey from meaning as problem to meaning as presence is the maturation of consciousness. You stop looking for your life's purpose and begin living purposefully—present, responsive, awake to what is.

As you move into Domain Nine, time itself becomes the teacher. You will discover that the past and future are not fixed realities but fluid movements within eternal presence, and that freedom lives not in controlling time but in seeing through it.

Domain Nine

The River of Becoming

Time, Choice, and the Eternal Now

Time is the most intimate illusion. It feels so real—the past trailing behind, the future rushing forward, this fleeting instant called "now" barely held before it vanishes. Yet when you look directly at time, it disappears.

- Where is the past? In memory—thought arising now.
- Where is the future? In imagination—thought arising now.
- Where is the present? Here, always here, never not here.

This domain explores the paradox of temporal existence: you live in time while being timeless. You make choices while flowing within currents you didn't create. You are both the river and the one carried by it.

The questions here are ancient: Do I have free will, or is everything predetermined? Am I creating my life, or is life living itself through me? The answer is not one or the other—it is both, simultaneously, depending on the depth from which you see.

Spring — Awakening to Flow

The Season of Current

Spring reveals life as movement. Not static being but dynamic becoming—everything arising, changing, dissolving. You are not a fixed point moving through time; you are time itself, flowing.

When you stop resisting this flow, something extraordinary happens: effort gives way to alignment. You discover that life has momentum, intelligence, direction—and you can either fight it or move with it.

The Triadic Lens

- **The River of Time**

  You cannot step in the same river twice—Heraclitus knew this. Everything flows. The self you were a moment ago is already gone. The world you inhabit is never the same twice. When you see this, clinging becomes absurd. There is nothing to hold; everything is already moving.

- **Synchronistic Awareness**

  Noticing meaningful coincidence—events that align not through causation but through resonance. Life speaking to itself through pattern. When you pay attention, the world begins to feel less random and more conversational.

- **The I Ching (Book of Changes)**

  Reality as dynamic interplay between yin and yang, stillness and movement, receptivity and action. Every moment is a hexagram—a particular configuration of forces. Wisdom is sensing which force is ascending and which is descending, then moving accordingly.

Experiencing the Lens

Sit by water if you can—a river, stream, or even rain falling. If not, close your eyes and imagine flowing water.

Notice: the water never stops. It does not ask if it should flow or where it should go. It simply follows the path of least resistance, endlessly moving.

Now feel your breath. Like water, it flows—in, out, in, out. You do not will this; it happens. Your heart beats. Your cells regenerate. Life flows through you without your permission.

Bring to mind a recent event that seemed like "coincidence"—an unexpected encounter, perfect timing, something that made you pause and think *that's strange*. Feel how this event arrived not through your planning but through the confluence of countless currents beyond your control.

This is synchronicity: life organizing itself in a meaningful way. When you notice it, you begin to sense that you are not isolated will imposing itself on inert matter. You are part of an intelligent field that moves through pattern, timing, and resonance.

Applications

- **In Daily Life**: When plans fall apart, ask: *What is the river showing me?* Often what seems like obstacle is redirection. The flow has intelligence; trust it.
- **In Relationship**: Notice how people appear in your life exactly when needed—not always who you expected, but who serves your becoming. Pay attention to these arrivals; they are rarely random.
- **In Inner Work**: Practice wu wei—effortless action. Choose one task and do it without forcing, without resisting. Let the doing happen through you rather than by you. Feel the difference between effort and flow.

The Koan

Am I moving, or is the river moving me?

Summer — The Fire of Choice

The Season of Will

Summer burns with agency. If Spring reveals the current, Summer reveals the one who navigates it. You are not passive leaf drifting—you are consciousness, capable of choice, able to redirect energy, to say yes or no.

Free will is not about controlling outcomes; it is about responding consciously rather than mechanically. When awareness is present, choice becomes creative rather than compulsive.

The Triadic Lens

- **Conscious Agency**

  The recognition that even within constraints, freedom exists. You cannot choose what arises, but you can choose how you meet what arises. Between stimulus and response, there is space—and in that space, will.

- **Decisional Clarity**

  Learning to choose from presence rather than from fear, habit, or conditioning. Clear choice feels different in the body—it arises from stillness, not agitation.

- **Existentialism (Sartre, Kierkegaard)**

  "Existence precedes essence." You are not born with a fixed nature—you create yourself through choices. This is both burden and freedom. Every decision is an act of self-creation.

Experiencing the Lens

Recall a moment when you made a choice that changed your life's trajectory—leaving a job, ending or beginning a relationship, moving to a new place.

Feel into that moment: What moved you to choose? Was it clear, or confused? Did it feel like freedom or compulsion?

Notice: even if the choice was difficult, there was a moment of *yes* or *no*—a decisive shift. That is will.

Now bring attention to a choice you face right now, small or large. Before deciding, feel into your body. Where is the yes? Where is the no?

The mind may argue, justify, explain—but the body already knows. Clarity lives beneath thinking. When you choose from that clarity, the decision carries energy. When you choose against it, you feel the cost.

This is the practice: learning to sense the difference between authentic choice and reactive habit. Will matures not through more control but through deeper listening.

Applications

- **In Daily Life**: Before making decisions, pause. Feel into the options. Which one opens space in your chest? Which one contracts? Let the body guide.
- **In Relationship**: Notice when you act from obligation versus genuine desire. Both are choices, but they carry different energy. One depletes; the other sustains.
- **In Inner Work**: Practice conscious choosing in small things. Tea or coffee? Walk or sit? Each tiny choice is an opportunity to be present with agency. Will is trained through attention, not force.

The Koan

Who chooses when the choice is clear?

Autumn — The Weaving of Destiny

The Season of Pattern

Autumn integrates Spring and Summer—flow and will, current and navigation. You see that your life is neither predetermined nor random. It is co-created: you and the universe, agency and allowance, intention and grace.

Destiny is not fate. It is the pattern of your becoming, visible only in retrospect. What seemed like an accident reveals itself as preparation. What felt like a detour was actually the path.

The Triadic Lens

- **Synchronicity (Jung)**

    Meaningful coincidence—when inner and outer align without a causal connection. Synchronicity suggests the psyche and world are not separate but two expressions of one reality.

- **Pattern Recognition**

    Seeing how themes repeat, how certain encounters recur, how your life has coherence when viewed as whole. The pattern is destiny revealing itself through time.

- **The Hermetic Principle "As Above, So Below"**

    Microcosm reflects macrocosm. Your personal life mirrors universal patterns. When you align with these patterns—cycles, seasons, rhythms—life becomes less struggle and more dance.

Experiencing the Lens

Map your life as if it were a story with chapters. What were the turning points? The moments that changed everything?

Now look for patterns. Do specific themes repeat? Do you return to similar lessons, similar struggles, similar breakthroughs?

This is not coincidence—it is the soul's curriculum. What keeps returning is what asks for integration.

Notice also: who appeared exactly when you needed them? What opportunities opened at the precise moment you were ready?

This is destiny—not imposed from outside but emerging from the interaction between your choices and life's intelligence. You are both author and character, writing and being written.

Applications

- **In Daily Life**: When obstacles arise, ask: *What pattern is this part of?* Often, what frustrates you is exactly what you need to grow through. Resistance is curriculum.
- **In Relationship**: Notice how certain people appear as teachers—sometimes through love, sometimes through friction. Each reflects something that is asking to be seen or healed in you.
- **In Inner Work**: Review your life as sacred text. Every event holds meaning when seen through awareness. The narrative is destiny speaking. Listen.

The Koan

Is my life happening to me, or as me?

Winter — The Eternal Now

The Season of Timelessness

Winter dissolves time. Past and future collapse into presence, and you discover that now is not a moment between what was and what will be—it is the only reality.

This does not deny change or cling to permanence. It is recognizing that change itself happens here, in this eternal instant. Time is not a container you move through; it is an appearance within the timeless.

The Triadic Lens

- **The Eternal Present**

    All experience occurs now. Memory is present thought about the past. Anticipation is present thought about the future. Only this—this breath, this awareness—is actual.

- **Presence Beyond Time**

    Resting as the awareness that never enters or leaves time. Thoughts come and go in time; awareness is timeless.

- **The Bhagavad Gita**

    "Your right is to action alone, never to its fruits." Act fully in the present without attachment to outcome. When you release the future, presence becomes total.

Experiencing the Lens

Close your eyes and feel the weight of your body, the rhythm of breath. This is now.

Try to find the past. Where is it? In memory—which is thought arising now.

Try to find the future. Where is it? In imagination—which is thought arising now.

Everything you have ever experienced, you experience now. Everything you will ever experience, you will experience now. There is only this—awareness meeting appearance, presence aware of itself.

Notice: when you rest here, time does not disappear. Clocks still tick, seasons still turn. But you are no longer in time—you are the space in which time appears.

This is freedom: not controlling what happens, but being so present that what happens is met fully, without the overlay of past or the anxiety of future.

Applications

- **In Daily Life**: When rushing, pause. Feel your feet. Notice breath. You cannot be late for now. Time pressure is thought; presence is fact.
- **In Relationship**: Be with others without reference to history or expectation. Meet them fresh, as if for the first time. This is love unburdened by time.
- **In Inner Work**: Let meditation be simply this: aware, now. Not becoming present—you cannot be anything but present. Simply recognizing what has always been true.

The Koan

What remains when time ends?

_____
_____
_____
_____
_____
_____
_____
_____

Closing Reflection on Domain Nine

Time is the river; you are both water and the one who watches it flow. Will is not separate from destiny—it is destiny becoming conscious of itself, making choices that were always already moving toward this moment.

Through these lenses, you discovered:

- How life flows with intelligence beyond your planning (Spring)
- How consciousness shapes reality through choice (Summer)
- How pattern weaves personal and universal into one story (Autumn)
- How all of time exists within the eternal now (Winter)

The paradox dissolves when you stop trying to resolve it: you are free within the flow, choosing within what is already unfolding, making meaning within what already matters.

As you enter Domain Ten, the mind's need for resolution itself becomes the focus. You will explore how paradox is not confusion but the signature of truth, and how opposites reveal themselves as partners in the dance of becoming.

Domain Ten

The Dance of Opposites

Paradox as Portal

Reality does not obey the mind's demand for consistency. Light is both wave and particle. You are both someone and no one. Freedom requires discipline. Love includes letting go.

The rational mind recoils from paradox, seeing contradiction as error. But mature awareness recognizes that truth is too large for logic—it requires holding opposites without collapsing them into false unity or splitting them into war.

This domain trains the capacity for paradoxical consciousness: seeing how what appears contradictory is actually complementary, how tension between opposites generates the energy of transformation, how the deepest truths are always both/and rather than either/or.

The goal is not to resolve paradox but to inhabit it—to become spacious enough that contradictions can coexist, creating friction that illuminates rather than destroys.

Spring — Opening to Paradox

The Season of Both/And

Spring reveals what the mind resists: opposites belong together. Day needs night. Strength requires vulnerability. To hold one side without the other is to fragment reality.

The Triadic Lens

- **Polarity Thinking**

  Recognizing that most tensions are not problems to solve but polarities to navigate. Independence and intimacy. Structure and freedom. Rest and motion. Each pole needs its opposite to be whole.

- **Dialectical Awareness**

  Holding thesis and antithesis without rushing to synthesis. Letting contradictions speak to each other until a third understanding emerges organically.

- **The Tao (Yin-Yang)**

  Each contains the seed of the other. Day turns to night; night becomes day. The movement between opposites is not conflict but collaboration—reality breathing in and out.

Experiencing the Lens

Notice where you live in either/or thinking. I'm either disciplined or spontaneous. Relationships are either close or distant. Life is either meaningful or empty.

Now feel the cost of this splitting. When you reject one pole to embrace the other, energy collapses. Life becomes rigid, flat.

Choose one polarity active in your life—perhaps control and surrender, speaking and silence, giving and receiving.

Instead of choosing, hold both. Feel control in your body—where does it live? Now feel surrender. Notice: they're not enemies. Control without surrender is rigidity. Surrender without control is chaos.

The dance between them is life. Let them move.

Applications

- **In Daily Life**: When you feel pulled between two options, stop treating it as a problem. Feel into both—what does each offer? Often, the answer is rhythm, not resolution.
- **In Relationship**: Notice how you oscillate between closeness and distance. This is not failure—it's breath. Inhale connection; exhale space. Both necessary.
- **In Inner Work**: Sit with a koan that holds paradox: *What is the sound of one hand clapping?* Let the contradiction undo the mind's certainty.

The Koan

Which wing does the bird need to fly?

Summer — The Fire of Integration

The Season of Wholeness

Summer shows how opposites complete each other. What seemed contradictory reveals itself as complementary—two faces of one truth.

The Triadic Lens

- **Complementarity**

  From quantum physics: wave and particle are not contradictory but context-dependent expressions of one reality. Consciousness works the same way—individual and universal, form and emptiness, depending on how you look.

- **Integrative Cognition**

  Synthesizing multiple perspectives without reducing them. Holding complexity without fragmentation.

- **The Middle Way (Buddha)**

  Not compromise between extremes but transcendence of the opposition itself. Neither attachment nor aversion. Neither eternalism nor nihilism. The path that includes both shores by recognizing the river.

Experiencing the Lens

Bring to mind two qualities you thought were incompatible—perhaps joy and sorrow, power and tenderness, certainty and doubt.

Feel into one, then the other. Now let them exist simultaneously.

Joy that knows sorrow is deeper. Power that includes tenderness is sustainable. Certainty that allows doubt remains open.

The integration is not blending—each remains distinct. But they stop fighting. They begin conversing.

Applications

- **In Daily Life**: Practice saying "and" instead of "but." Not "I love you, but I need space"—rather "I love you, and I need space." Feel how "and" holds both truths without negating either.
- **In Relationship**: Stop trying to be consistent. You can be confident and uncertain, generous and boundaried, devoted and independent. Wholeness includes contradictions.
- **In Inner Work**: When meditation feels contradictory—effort and effortlessness, focus and openness—stop choosing. Be both. This is the middle way.

The Koan

Can emptiness be full?

Autumn — Holding the Tension

The Season of Crucible

Autumn teaches that tension is creative. The friction between opposites generates heat, and heat transforms. This is the alchemical fire—not comfort, but the productive discomfort that refines.

The Triadic Lens

- **Dynamic Equilibrium**

  Balance through movement, not stasis. Like a tightrope walker adjusting constantly, never still but always centered.

- **Holding Paradox**

  Developing the musculature to sustain contradiction without collapse or premature resolution. Tension is the teacher.

- **Hegelian Dialectic**

  Thesis, antithesis, synthesis—but synthesis is not endpoint. It becomes new thesis, inviting new antithesis. Evolution through contradiction.

Experiencing the Lens

Find a place in your life where two truths collide—wanting stability and craving change, needing connection and valuing solitude, pursuing goals and surrendering to flow.

Feel the tension. Do not resolve it. Just hold both.

The mind wants to choose, to decide, to end the discomfort. Don't. Stay in the tension like holding a yoga pose—uncomfortable but strengthening.

What emerges when you don't force resolution? Often, a third possibility neither side could see alone.

Applications

- **In Daily Life**: When facing difficult choices, resist deciding too quickly. Live the question. The tension itself clarifies.

- **In Relationship**: When values conflict—yours and another's—hold both as valid. Tension is not failure; it's depth. Real intimacy includes unresolved difference.
- **In Inner Work**: Notice when you try to eliminate inner conflict. Instead, let the parts speak to each other. The dialogue is transformation.

The Koan

What births in the space between yes and no?

Winter — Beyond Duality

The Season of Unity

Winter dissolves the distinction between opposites. Not by erasing difference but by revealing the ground from which both arise.

The Triadic Lens

- **Nondual Awareness**

  The recognition that all opposites are movements of one reality. Light and dark, self and other, being and nonbeing—distinctions made by mind, not separations in truth.

- **Trans-logical Knowing**

  Beyond logic's either/or, even beyond both/and. Simply *this*—reality before division, awareness prior to category.

- **Advaita (Not-Two)**

  Neither one nor many. Not monism, not dualism. The dissolution of the question itself.

Experiencing the Lens

Sit and notice breathing. In and out are opposites—yet they're one continuous movement.

Notice heartbeat—contraction and release, two phases of one pulse.

Notice awareness—subject perceiving objects—yet when you look, where is the boundary?

Let opposites dissolve. Not into confusion but into simplicity. The distinctions remain—you still know in from out, light from dark—but they no longer divide.

Everything arises in the same field. Everything returns to the same source. The dance of opposites is consciousness exploring itself.

Rest here. No paradox to solve. No tension to hold. Just the seamless presence that contains all contradiction without being touched by any.

Applications

- **In Daily Life**: When opposites appear—success/failure, pleasure/pain—see them as weather. Different conditions, same sky.
- **In Relationship**: The apparent boundary between self and other—feel how porous it is. Different bodies, one awareness. The separation is functional, not fundamental.
- **In Inner Work**: Let practice become so simple there's nothing to practice. No meditator, no meditation. Just awareness being what it has always been.

The Koan

Where is the line between wave and ocean?

Closing Reflection on Domain Ten

Paradox is not confusion—it is reality showing its full face. When the mind stops demanding consistency, awareness discovers that truth is larger than logic, more fluid than definition.

Through these lenses:

- Opposites revealed themselves as partners (Spring)
- Integration showed how contradictions complete each other (Summer)
- Tension became the crucible of transformation (Autumn)
- Duality dissolved into the simplicity of what is (Winter)

The dance continues—form and emptiness, stillness and motion, silence and sound—but you are no longer caught in choosing sides. You rest as the space that holds all movement, the awareness that contains all opposites without becoming any of them.

As you enter Domain Eleven, even the dance begins to quiet. You will discover that awakening is not achievement but surrender, that the door you've been seeking has no lock, and that freedom comes not through gaining but through the exhaustion of seeking itself.

Domain Eleven

The Door with No Key

Effortless Realization

There comes a moment when seeking exhausts itself, not through finding what was sought, but through recognizing the futility of seeking what was never lost.

Every path leads here eventually: to the realization that awakening is not attained—it is recognized. The one who would awaken is the only obstacle to awakening. When that one dissolves, what remains is what has always been: simple, obvious, already complete.

This domain is the quieting of effort. Not collapse into passivity, but the discovery that awareness does not require your help to be aware. When you stop interfering, presence reveals itself as effortless—breathing you, seeing through you, living as you without needing your permission or participation.

The door has no key because there is no door. What you took to be a barrier was always a threshold—and you were always already through.

Spring — The Paradox of Effort

The Season of Loosening

Spring reveals the contradiction at the heart of practice: you cannot *try* to be present. Effort is the distraction.

The Triadic Lens

- **Wu Wei (Non-Doing)**
  Action without forcing. Not laziness but alignment—moving with reality's current rather than against it.

- **Surrender-Based Awareness**

  Letting awareness operate itself. You do not make yourself aware; awareness simply is. Your only work is stopping the interference.

- **The Gateless Gate (Mumonkan)**

  Zen's most famous collection of koans. Each one a gateless barrier—meaning the barrier exists only in your belief that there's something to pass through.

Experiencing the Lens

Sit and try—really try—to be present. Notice what happens: effort arises, which is thought, which takes you out of presence.

Now stop trying. Just be. Whatever is here—thought, sensation, stillness—let it be exactly as it is.

Feel the difference. Trying creates tension. Allowing creates space.

This is the paradox: you cannot become what you already are. Every effort to "get there" assumes you're somewhere else. However, awareness is always present, never absent.

Applications

- **In Daily Life**: When you notice striving toward presence, smile. That noticing is already presence. You've arrived by seeing you never left.
- **In Relationship**: Stop trying to be present with others. Simply be. The trying creates distance; the being dissolves it.
- **In Inner Work**: Let meditation be purposeless. Not sitting to achieve, but sitting because sitting is what's happening.

The Koan

Who is trying to awaken?

Summer — The Flow of Being

The Season of Spontaneity

Summer shows what happens when effort dissolves: action arises naturally, without the doer. Life moves through you like breath—effortless, responsive, alive.

The Triadic Lens

- **Spontaneous Presence**

    The recognition that when awareness is clear, appropriate action emerges without deliberation. You don't decide what to do—you feel what's needed and do it.

- **Embodied Flow**

    Movement arising from the body's intelligence rather than mental planning. The dancer disappears into dancing; the speaker disappears into speech.

- **Mushin (No-Mind)**

    The Zen archer who releases the arrow without deciding to shoot. Action and awareness are one movement.

Experiencing the Lens

Choose something simple—walking, washing dishes, making tea. Do it without narrating, without planning the next step.

Let the body move itself. The hand knows how to reach. The feet know how to step. Awareness flows through action without commentary.

Notice: when thought is absent, action is precise. The thinking mind complicates; the clear mind simply responds.

Applications

- **In Daily Life**: Let one activity each day be completely spontaneous. No rehearsal, no agenda. Trust what arises.
- **In Relationship**: Speak without preparing. Listen without formulating response. Let conversation be jazz—improvised, alive.

- **In Inner Work:** When insight arises, don't grab it or try to remember it. Let it move through like everything else. What remains is what matters.

The Koan

What acts when no one is acting?

Autumn — The Trust of Surrender

The Season of Release

Autumn deepens the realization: you are not in control, and that is grace. Life unfolds with or without your permission. When you stop resisting this, the burden lifts.

The Triadic Lens

- **Radical Trust**

  Not blind faith but intelligent recognition: awareness knows what to do. The body knows how to heal. Life knows how to live itself.

- **Intuitive Yielding**

  Sensing when to act and when to wait, when to push and when to allow. This is not passivity—it is participation in something larger than will.

- **The Serenity Prayer (Reinhold Niebuhr)**

  "Grant me the serenity to accept what I cannot change, courage to change what I can, and wisdom to know the difference." The wisdom is recognizing that most of what you try to control was never yours to control.

Experiencing the Lens

Reflect on something you've been trying to make happen—a relationship, a career shift, a personal change.

Feel the effort, the pushing. Now ask: *What if this isn't mine to control?*

Not resignation but release. Feel the difference in your body—how much energy was going into forcing.

Now sense: what *is* yours? Your presence. Your response. Your willingness to be with what is. That's all. And that's enough.

Applications

- **In Daily Life**: When you catch yourself forcing—an outcome, an understanding, a feeling—stop. Breathe. Ask what happens if you let go.

- **In Relationship**: Trust that you don't need to manage others' feelings or fix their process. Your presence is the gift; their journey is theirs.
- **In Inner Work**: Stop trying to have the "right" experience in meditation. Whatever arises is what's here. Trust that.

The Koan

What remains when control is released?

Winter — The Simplicity of What Is

The Season of Naturalness

Winter dissolves even surrender. There is no one surrendering, no effort to release effort. Only this—awareness being what it has always been, needing nothing, lacking nothing, complete.

The Triadic Lens

- **Natural Awareness**

    Awareness that requires no cultivation, no maintenance, no achievement. It is simply here—like sky, like space, always present.

- **Effortless Recognition**

    Not arriving at understanding but noticing what was always obvious. The search ends not in finding but in seeing that what was sought was the seeker.

- **Dzogchen—Self-Liberation Through Seeing**

    Every experience liberates itself upon being seen. Thought arises and dissolves, unmodified by awareness. The mirror remains clear regardless of what appears in it.

Experiencing the Lens

Stop.

Don't do anything. Don't even try to be present.

Notice: awareness is already here. It has never not been here. It requires nothing from you.

Thoughts come and go—awareness remains.

Breath moves—awareness remains.

Body sensations arise—awareness remains.

You are this. Not the thoughts, not the sensations—the awareness that knows them. And awareness is effortless. It doesn't try to be aware; it simply is.

Rest here. Not because you should, but because there's nowhere else to be.

Applications
- **In Daily Life**: Whenever you remember, pause and recognize: *I am aware.* Not as practice but as fact. This recognition is itself freedom.
- **In Relationship**: See that the awareness in you and in them is not two. The same light, looking through different eyes.
- **In Inner Work**: Let practice dissolve into being. The work is done. What remains is living.

The Koan

What was never lost?

Closing Reflection on Domain Eleven

The door opens not because you found the key but because you stopped believing in the lock. Awakening is not distant—it is the simple recognition that effort obscures what is already free.

Through these lenses:

- Effort revealed itself as the obstacle (Spring)
- Spontaneity emerged when doing dissolved (Summer)
- Trust replaced control (Autumn)
- Natural awareness was seen to be always present (Winter)

Nothing was achieved because nothing was missing. The work of this domain is not transformation but transparency—seeing through the illusion that you need to become other than what you are.

As you move into Domain Twelve, even seeing becomes self-seeing. Awareness recognizes that it has always been both the light and what the light illuminates—consciousness beholding itself through infinite forms, the Eye seeing its seeing.

Domain Twelve

The Eye That Sees Itself

Consciousness Recognizing Consciousness

Every perception you've ever had was awareness knowing itself. Every thought, sensation, emotion—all of it was consciousness appearing to itself, the infinite taking form to experience its own nature.

For most of life, awareness looks outward. It perceives objects, experiences states, and navigates the world of appearance. But there comes a turning—subtle, profound—when awareness bends back upon itself and recognizes: *I am what I have been seeking.*

This is not philosophical insight. It is direct recognition—the moment the eye sees itself, not as reflection but as the seeing itself. When this occurs, the search ends. Not because something is found, but because the distinction between seeker and sought dissolves.

This domain is the completion of perception's journey. What began as learning to see freshly ends in the recognition that all seeing is consciousness beholding its own light.

Spring — Awareness of Awareness

The Season of Turning

Spring marks the first reversal: instead of being aware *of* something, you become aware *of being aware*. Attention turns from the object to the knowing of the object.

The Triadic Lens

- **Reflexive Consciousness**

  Awareness aware of itself. This is not circular—it is the natural luminosity of consciousness, which knows itself by being itself.

- Self-Inquiry

  The practice of turning attention toward the one who perceives. Not analyzing but recognizing—who is here before thought, beneath sensation, prior to experience?

- "Who Am I?" (Ramana Maharshi)

  The question that dissolves the questioner. Each time you ask, identity loosens. What remains is the silence that was always listening.

Experiencing the Lens

Notice that you are aware. Not aware *of* anything in particular—just the bare fact: awareness is present.

Now ask: *Who is aware?*

When an answer arises—*I am aware*—notice that "I" is thought appearing in awareness. It is not the answer.

Ask again: *Who is aware of the thought "I"?*

Each time you turn attention back, you find only space—vast, luminous, without center or edge. This space is not empty. It is the fullness of awareness itself.

You cannot see awareness as an object because you *are* awareness. You are not looking *at* it—you are looking *as* it.

Applications

- **In Daily Life**: Throughout the day, pause and recognize: *I am aware.* Not "I am aware of this"—just the simple fact of being conscious.
- **In Relationship**: Notice that the awareness in you and the awareness in another are not separate. Different forms, one light.
- **In Inner Work**: Begin meditation by asking, "Who am I?" Let the question undo every answer until only silence remains.

The Koan

Who is aware of awareness?

Summer — The Light of Recognition

The Season of Radiance

Summer brings the realization that awareness is self-luminous. It does not need anything outside itself to be known. Like fire, which illuminates and *is* light, awareness knows and *is* knowing.

The Triadic Lens

- **Self-Luminous Consciousness**

  Awareness is not lit by something else—it is light itself. Every experience shines because awareness illuminates it from within.

- **Direct Perception**

  Knowing without mediation. Before thought names, before mind interprets—pure contact between awareness and appearance.

- **Rigpa (Dzogchen)**

  Primordial awareness—self-arising, self-knowing, never absent. Not a state to achieve, but the ground of all states.

Experiencing the Lens

Sit quietly and notice: you are aware of the body, aware of sounds, aware of thoughts. But what makes these knowable?

Awareness itself. Without it, nothing appears. Yet awareness itself cannot be seen as object—it is the seeing.

This is self-luminosity: awareness reveals everything, including itself, by being what it is. It requires no external light because it *is* light.

Feel into this: the knowing of experience is not separate from experience. Awareness and appearance arise together—neither first, neither second.

When this is seen, the world becomes transparent. Every form is awareness appearing as form, every sensation is consciousness touching itself.

Applications

- **In Daily Life**: See that everything you perceive is consciousness manifesting. The tree, the hand, the breath—all are awareness taking shape.
- **In Relationship**: Recognize the same awareness looking through every eye. Not as belief but as direct seeing.
- **In Inner Work**: Rest in the recognition that awareness needs no cultivation. It is already fully present, fully radiant.

The Koan

What shines before the sun rises?

Autumn — The Dissolution of Division

The Season of Unity

Autumn reveals what Summer illuminated: there is no boundary between awareness and what it knows. Subject and object, perceiver and perceived—these are conceptual divisions within a seamless field.

The Triadic Lens

- **Nondual Perception**

  The recognition that all duality is appearance within unity. Not one thing, not two things—just this, exactly as it is.

- **Trans-Categorical Knowing**

  Beyond subject and object, beyond one and many. The mind's categories dissolve into direct recognition.

- **Madhyamaka (Nagarjuna)**

  The Middle Way—neither existence nor non-existence. All distinctions are empty of inherent reality, yet conventionally valid like waves and ocean—distinct and inseparable.

Experiencing the Lens

Look at your hand. Notice: there is seeing, and there is the hand. Where is the boundary between them?

When you search for it, you find none. The seeing and the seen arise together, neither possible without the other.

Now broaden this: hear a sound. Where does the hearing end and the sound begin? Feel a sensation. Where does awareness stop and sensation start?

The division is conceptual, not actual. In direct experience, there is only one continuous field—awareness appearing as world, world dissolving into awareness.

Rest in this recognition. You are not inside looking out. You are the entire field—seeing and seen, knowing and known, all arising in the same space.

Applications

- **In Daily Life**: When the sense of "in here" and "out there" appears, feel for the boundary. Let it soften until experience becomes seamless.
- **In Relationship**: The apparent separation between self and other is functional, not fundamental. Feel the field that includes both.
- **In Inner Work**: Let meditation dissolve into non-meditation. No one sitting, no practice happening. Just awareness, being.

The Koan

Where does the mirror end and the reflection begin?

Winter — The Silence Beyond Seeing

The Season of Completion

Winter is the quietest teaching: when the eye sees itself completely, even "seeing" dissolves. What remains is so simple it cannot be named—awareness resting as itself, prior to all division, including the division between knowing and not knowing.

The Triadic Lens

- **Pure Consciousness Without Object**

   Awareness prior to experience. Not void but fullness—infinite potential before manifestation.

- **Non-Conceptual Recognition**

   Beyond thought, beyond perception, beyond even awareness of awareness. The ground of all, holding all, being all.

- **"Tat Tvam Asi" (Thou Art That)**

   The great utterance from the Upanishads. The essence of you and the essence of all reality are not two. This is not conclusion—it is recognition.

Experiencing the Lens

Let everything fall away.

Not the things themselves—they remain. But your relationship to them. No grasping, no rejecting, no observing.

Just this.

Breath happening.

Sound appearing.

Awareness being.

No one here doing any of it.

No one here experiencing any of it.

Just the happening.

This is not emptiness—it is too full for that. It is not presence—that word is too small. It is what is before naming begins, what remains after naming ends.

You cannot understand this. You can only be it. And you already are.

Applications

- **In Daily Life**: When you remember, stop. Not to become present but to recognize you've never been absent.
- **In Relationship**: Let all roles dissolve. Not teacher, not student, not self, not other. Just awareness meeting itself in form.
- **In Inner Work**: There is no work. There never was. Only awareness, appearing as the one who works, appearing as the work itself.

The Koan

What was your face before your parents were born?

Closing Reflection on Domain Twelve

The eye sees itself, and in that seeing, realizes it was never separate from what it saw. Consciousness recognizes consciousness—not as achievement but as the nature of being itself.

Through these lenses:

- Awareness became aware of itself (Spring)
- Recognition revealed self-luminosity (Summer)
- All division dissolved into unity (Autumn)
- Even seeing released into pure being (Winter)

This is not the end—it is the return to the beginning, now transparent. The circle completes, yet has no edge. The one who began this journey and the one who arrives are both seen as appearances within what never moved.

As you enter the final domain, even completion dissolves. The Transparent Circle reveals that the entire journey was consciousness playing with itself—creating questions only to discover the questioner, building paths only to find they led nowhere because there was nowhere to go.

Domain Thirteen

The Transparent Circle

The Return to Source

You have traveled through twelve domains, forty-eight lenses. You have learned to see, to question, to feel, to embody, to relate, to integrate shadow, to witness thought, to discover meaning, to move with time, to hold paradox, to surrender effort, and to know yourself as the eye that sees.

Now there is only return.

Not return as repetition, but as recognition. The circle does not close—it was never open. What you sought has been here all along, so obvious it could not be seen. The journey was not toward something distant but into the heart of what is.

Transparency is not a state to achieve. It is what remains when all doing dissolves, when the seeker and the sought are recognized as one movement, one breath, one light.

In this final domain, words thin to silence. The teaching points beyond itself and disappears. What you have practiced becomes what you are—not something you do, but the simplicity of being.

The circle breathes you. And in that breath, you have changed the way you see everything—not by gaining new eyes, but by recognizing you are the seeing.

Spring — The Gateless Gate

The Season of Opening

There is a gate that has no gate. A door that cannot be entered because you are already inside.

The spiritual path promises arrival—someday, after enough practice, enough purification, you will reach the destination. But this is the final illusion. There is nowhere to arrive. You are already what you seek.

The Triadic Lens

- Non-Attainment

    Nothing can be gained because nothing was lost. The Buddha's awakening was not the acquisition of enlightenment but the recognition that the self who sought it never existed. The goal is the obstacle. When seeking ends, what was always here reveals itself.

- Negative Theology

    The via negativa—the path of negation. You cannot say what the Real is, only what it is not. Not this, not that. Neti neti. Each denial strips away a layer of concept until language fails, leaving direct knowing.

- Zen Mu (No-Gate)

    The koan is the question with no answer. It cannot be solved by thought. It can only be lived into—again and again—until the mind exhausts itself and something else opens. The gateless gate is not a puzzle to crack but a recognition to embody: I am what I was seeking.

Experiencing the Lens

Sit and feel the familiar impulse to become something—calmer, clearer, more present, more awake. Notice how this wanting creates the very distance it seeks to close.

Now ask: What if there is nothing to attain?

Not as philosophy but as direct inquiry. Feel into the possibility that awareness is already complete, that nothing needs to be added or removed, that the seeker is the sought, wearing the mask of separation.

Let effort dissolve, not through force, but through seeing its futility. The gate opens not when you find the right key, but when you realize the lock was never fastened.

Applications
- **In Daily Life**: Notice when you tell yourself, "When I'm less stressed, then I'll be present" or "When I finish this, then I'll rest." The condition is the problem. What if you are already what you're waiting to become?
- **In Relationship**: Stop trying to be seen. You are the seeing. Stop trying to be loved. You are the love meeting itself in another's eyes.
- **In Inner Work**: Abandon the project of self-improvement. Not because you're perfect, but because the one trying to improve is a fiction. Who you actually are needs no improvement.

The Koan

What stands between you and what you already are?

Summer — The Fire of Dissolution

The Season of Illumination

Summer burns. Not to destroy, but to reveal. What cannot withstand fire was never real.

All practices, all teachings, all paths point here: to the moment when structure collapses, and only essence remains. This is not loss—it is liberation. The scaffolding falls away, and the temple stands free.

The Triadic Lens

- **Kenosis (Self-Emptying)**

    From Christian mysticism: the complete pouring out of self until only divine presence remains. Not annihilation but transfiguration. The drop does not become the ocean—it recognizes it was always the ocean appearing as a drop.

- **Apophatic Awareness**

    Awareness known through absence. When every concept of who you are dissolves—body, mind, role, history, future—what remains? This remainder is not nothing. It is the ground of everything, too simple to be grasped, too intimate to be lost.

- **The Dark Night as Illumination**

    What mystics called the dark night—the stripping away of all consolation, all certainty—is not punishment but grace. When every support collapses, you discover you need no support. When every light goes out, you find you are the light.

Experiencing the Lens

Bring attention to the sense of being someone—the felt identity, the continuous "I" that threads through experience.

Now ask: What if this dissolves?

Not as death but as transparency. The "I" was never a thing—it was a movement of awareness, consciousness creating the appearance of a center where there is only openness.

Let the familiar sense of self soften, not through effort, but through attention. See how "I" arises moment to moment, always fresh, never solid. Thought says "I." Sensation says "I." Memory says "I." But who is speaking?

Rest in the space before "I" forms. Here, there is awareness, but no one aware. Presence but no person present. This is not emptiness—it is fullness too vast to be contained in identity.

Applications

- **In Daily Life**: When you catch yourself defending who you are—your beliefs, your story, your rightness—pause. What if you don't need to be anyone at all? Not as resignation but as freedom.
- **In Relationship**: Let yourself be unseen. Not hidden, but transparent. When you stop performing identity, intimacy becomes possible.
- **In Inner Work**: Stop trying to fix, improve, or transcend the self. Instead, investigate: Is there actually a self to fix? Look for the one who needs healing and discover there's only healing happening, no one to be healed.

The Koan

Who remains when the fire goes out?

Autumn — The Integration of Nothing

The Season of Integration

You cannot integrate nothing. But you can recognize that nothing was ever separate.

Autumn is the season of return—not to where you started, but to what was always here beneath the journey. Wisdom does not accumulate; it ripens through letting go. What remains is simpler than what was sought.

The Triadic Lens

- **Nondual Recognition**

  Not-two. The opposites that structured your search—self and other, inner and outer, sacred and mundane—were never divided. They are one reality appearing as two. To see this is not to gain a view but to lose the need for views.

- **Integrative Collapse**

  The mind tries to integrate awakening into life, as if they were separate. But there is no life apart from awakening, no awakening apart from life. Trying to integrate them creates the split. When effort stops, they are discovered to be the same movement.

- **Ordinary Mind Is the Way**

  Zen teaching: enlightenment is not special. It is the simple ease of being—chopping wood, carrying water, laughing, weeping. When the search ends, the ordinary becomes luminous. There was never anything to transcend.

Experiencing the Lens

Notice how spiritual practice creates a subtle hierarchy: meditation is sacred, email is mundane. Silence is profound, conversation is distraction.

Now let this collapse. What if washing dishes is as sacred as sitting zazen? What if the breath you take while reading this is as immediate as any mystical vision?

Feel the relief in this recognition. You don't need to escape life to find the Real. You don't need to transcend the body, quiet the mind, or perfect the heart. You only need to be here—fully, simply here.

This is not settling. It is arrival. The treasure was buried in your own backyard. You dug for years in distant lands only to return and find it waiting where you started.

Applications

- **In Daily Life**: Stop dividing experience into spiritual and unspiritual. Traffic is as much the dharma as dawn meditation. Your neighbor's complaint is as much a teaching as any sutra.
- **In Relationship**: See the divine in the difficult. Not as metaphor but as fact. The person who irritates you is God appearing as irritation, inviting you to meet what you reject.
- **In Inner Work**: Abandon the work. Not as laziness but as recognition. There is nothing to work on. The one you were trying to improve was a ghost. What you are is already whole.

The Koan

Where does the sacred begin?

_____
_____
_____
_____
_____
_____

Winter — The Breath of Silence

The Season of Dissolution

Silence is not the absence of sound. It is the presence before and beneath all sound—the space in which music arises, the stillness in which words dissolve.

You are this silence. Not the quiet between thoughts, but the vast awareness that holds both silence and sound without preferring either. This final lens is barely a lens at all. It is the seeing looking back at itself and finding no one there.

The Triadic Lens

- **The Unborn**

  What was never born cannot die. Awareness does not begin or end. It has no history, no future. It is always now, always here—the eternal witness that remains untouched by time.

- **Cessation of Concepts**

  Thought stops not through force but through completion. The mind, having exhausted every question, every answer, every path, falls silent. In that silence, everything is known without knowing. This is wisdom beyond wisdom—the unknowing that sees everything.

- **Mahamudra (The Great Seal)**

  The Tibetan teaching of resting in natural mind—effortless, uncontrived, free of all reference points. Nothing to do, nowhere to go, no one to become. The seal is already complete. You are already home.

Experiencing the Lens

Close your eyes. Feel breath moving—not as something you're doing, but as something being lived through you. The breath breathes itself.

Now notice: awareness is like this. It knows without trying. It is present without effort. There is no gap between you and awareness—you are awareness appearing as this body, this moment, this reading of words.

Let everything rest. Thought, sensation, identity, purpose—let it all settle like snow falling on still water. What remains is not an experience. It is the ground of all experience—formless, timeless, silent.

This is not a state to maintain. It is what you are beneath every state. Whether lost in thought or anchored in presence, whether suffering or serene, this awareness is constant. You cannot leave it because it is not a place. You cannot lose it because it is not a thing.

Simply rest as what you are. Not the body, though the body appears. Not the mind, though thoughts arise. You are the space itself—luminous, empty, complete.

Applications

There are no applications. There is only this.

The Koan

What word breaks the silence without disturbing it?

Closing Reflection on Domain Thirteen

The circle is complete because it was never broken.

You began seeking and have arrived at the seeker's dissolution. Not as tragedy but as homecoming. What you chased—peace, clarity, awakening, love—was the one chasing revealed to itself.

There is no final truth to state. Truth is the silence between these words. It is the breath you just took without thinking. It is the aware space reading this sentence.

Fifty-two lenses. One year. One lifetime. All to arrive where you always were—present, awake, transparent to the light that shines through all things.

This book dissolves now. It was only ever a finger pointing at the moon. You have looked long enough. The moon has seen you. You are the moon, the finger, the looking, and the light.

Nothing more needs to be said. Nothing more needs to be done. You are what you sought. Rest.

"The Tao that can be told is not the eternal Tao.
The name that can be named is not the eternal name.
The nameless is the beginning of heaven and earth."
— Tao Te Ching

"When I let go of what I am,
I become what I might be."
— Lao Tzu

---

*"Before enlightenment, chop wood, carry water.
After enlightenment, chop wood, carry water."*
— Zen saying

*The work is complete.
The circle breathes.
You are home.*

Afterword

The Circle Breathes You

The circle was never meant to be traveled, only remembered. Every path, every question, every lens you explored was the movement of awareness turning opening into itself. Now that you stand at what seems like the end, look carefully—there is no edge here. Only the transparency of being, endlessly wormholing into itself.

All that has been seen was the seeing itself. Every insight, every flame was the same awareness speaking in a different voice.

The alchemy is complete when you realize it never began. Awareness was not transformed; it revealed what was always true. The one who sought to awaken was the awakening all along.

The circle does not close; it breathes. With every breath, it expands as experience and contracts as silence. The inhalation is the world becoming you; the exhalation is you returning to the world. Between the two, there is no separation—only the pulse of one infinite presence expressing itself in rhythm.

You are not inside this awareness—you are its expression, its luminous pulse. The circle is you: transparent, indivisible, alive.

When the mind quiets, you may hear it: the silent exhalation of the cosmos, the eternal whisper:

"I am."

Let this be your practice, your prayer, your homecoming—not to arrive anywhere new, but to rest where you have always been.

The circle breathes you.

And in that breath, everything is complete.

Final Reflection

The Soul as the Lens of the Absolute

I was a treasure longing to be known, so I opened my eyes as you.

From the stillness of non-being, IT leaned into the shimmer of form, and the soul arose—a lens through which the Absolute could behold itself in motion.

The soul is not separate from the Infinite; it is the curvature of awareness bending into love. It gathers light into meaning, sound into silence, being into the whisper of "I am."

Yet even this is simplicity itself—simply this, suchness. No hidden code, no secret path, only the quiet miracle of what is here now.

Between the hush of non-being and the brilliance of being, there is only a breath—the pulse of not-knowing giving birth to revelation, emptiness flowering as form, form dissolving back into emptiness.

The eternal dance: nothing becoming everything, everything returning to nothing.

Space is not absence but intimacy—the openness through which all arises, the silent hospitality of the Absolute receiving itself. Within that infinite expanse, the soul gleams for an instant—transparent, trembling, aware—then falls gently back into the sea of its origin.

What remains is not silence, but the sound of silence listening to itself.

Not you, but the treasure—known, knowing, forever knowing itself anew.

52 Lenses

1. The Map Is Not the Territory - Beginner's Mind - The GROW Model
2. The Observer Effect - Critical Thinking - The Socratic Method
3. Cognitive Reframing - Metacognitive Reflection - Phenomenological Reduction (Epoché)
4. Pure Awareness - Direct Experience - Husserl's Epoché (Deepened)
5. Constructivism - Reflective Thinking - The Hero's Journey
6. The Looking-Glass Self - Narrative Thinking - The Enneagram
7. Cognitive Reframing - Metacognition - The Cognitive Triad
8. The Empty Self - Paradoxical Thinking - The Nondual View
9. Emotional Granularity - Experiential Awareness - The Window of Tolerance
10. Energy Conservation - Embodied Cognition - Polyvagal Theory
11. Emotional Transmutation - Somatic Reflection - The Felt Sense (Gendlin)
12. Equanimity - Contemplative Awareness - The Heart Sutra
13. Somatic Intelligence - Body-Mind Integration - Gurdjieff's Three Centers
14. Sensory Gnosis - Phenomenology of the Flesh (Merleau-Ponty) - The Tantric Body
15. Embodied Presence - Somatic Experiencing - The Body as a Mandala
16. The Body of Light - Dissolving into Space - The Diamond Body / Rainbow Body
17. Secure Base - Relational Awareness - The Circle of Security
18. Intersubjectivity - Resonance - Martin Buber's I-Thou
19. Projection - Shadow Work - The Imago Dialogue
20. Nondual Love - Unity Consciousness - The Beloved in All Forms (Sufi)
21. The Personal Shadow (Jung) - Compassionate Inquiry - The 3-2-1 Shadow Process (Integral)
22. The Golden Shadow - Both/And Consciousness - Active Imagination (Jung)
23. The Cultural Shadow - Archetypal Awareness - Scapegoating (René Girard)
24. Coincidentia Oppositorum - Nondual Embrace - The Dark Night of the Soul (St. John of the Cross)
25. Metacognition - Witnessing Awareness - Vipassana (Insight Meditation)
26. Thought as a Form of Energy - Flow States - The Hermetic Principle of Mentalism

27. The Gap in Consciousness - Resting Attention - Zen Shikantaza (Just Sitting)
28. Non-Conceptual Knowing - Direct Recognition - The Zen Koan
29. Existential Curiosity - Appreciative Inquiry - Logotherapy (Viktor Frankl)
30. Teleology - Intuitive Knowing - Ikigai (Japanese)
31. Existential Crisis as Initiation - Narrative Flexibility - The Hero's Journey (Revisited)
32. Being as Meaning - Contemplative Presence - The Tao Te Ching
33. The River of Time - Synchronistic Awareness - The I Ching (Book of Changes)
34. Conscious Agency - Decisional Clarity - Existentialism (Sartre, Kierkegaard)
35. Synchronicity (Jung) - Pattern Recognition - The Hermetic Principle "As Above, So Below"
36. The Eternal Present - Presence Beyond Time - The Bhagavad Gita
37. Polarity Thinking - Dialectical Awareness - The Tao (Yin-Yang)
38. Complementarity - Integrative Cognition - The Middle Way (Buddha)
39. Dynamic Equilibrium - Holding Paradox - Hegelian Dialectic
40. Nondual Awareness - Trans-logical Knowing - Advaita (Not-Two)
41. Wu Wei (Non-Doing) - Surrender-Based Awareness - The Gateless Gate (Mumonkan)
42. Spontaneous Presence - Embodied Flow - Mushin (No-Mind)
43. Radical Trust - Intuitive Yielding - The Serenity Prayer (Reinhold Niebuhr)
44. Natural Awareness - Effortless Recognition - Dzogchen—Self-Liberation Through Seeing
45. Reflexive Consciousness - Self-Inquiry - "Who Am I?" (Ramana Maharshi)
46. Self-Luminous Consciousness - Direct Perception - Rigpa (Dzogchen)
47. Nondual Perception - Trans-Categorical Knowing - Madhyamaka (Nagarjuna)
48. Pure Consciousness Without Object - Non-Conceptual Recognition - "Tat Tvam Asi" (Thou Art That)
49. Non-Attainment - Negative Theology - Zen Mu (No-Gate)
50. Kenosis (Self-Emptying) - Apophatic Awareness - The Dark Night as Illumination
51. Nondual Recognition - Integrative Collapse - Ordinary Mind Is the Way

52. The Unborn - Cessation of Concepts - Mahamudra (The Great Seal)

The Inner Architecture Trilogy

The three books in this trilogy form a single unfolding journey: from the machinery of personality, to the transformation of perception, to the living process that reveals who you truly are beneath the patterns. Each book stands alone, but together they create a seamless arc—how the self is formed, how it is seen, and how it is liberated.

> **Why Study Personality?** opens the door. It reveals the architecture of identity, the three centers, and the hidden workings of the mechanisms that shape your inner world before you ever knew you had one.
>
> **The Alchemy of Perception** deepens the descent. It shows how seeing is not passive but creative—how every moment is shaped by the way awareness meets experience. It refines the instrument of perception so the world can be encountered directly, without distortion.
>
> **The Enneagram as Living Process** completes the arc. It presents the Enneagram not as a typology but as a living map of consciousness—how Being moves, forgets itself, and remembers. It shows how personality arises as an interruption in a much larger rhythm, and how the same rhythm contains the way home.

Together, these books offer a unified approach to awakening:

- a psychology with a soul
- a spirituality grounded in experience
- a map that brings all three centers—mind, heart, and body—back into a single field of knowing.

This trilogy is for anyone who senses that personal growth is not about becoming a better version of the pattern, but about rediscovering the one who has never been defined by it.

It is a journey into the sacred science of sound—the unstruck melodies, cosmic vibrations, and primordial tones that shape reality.

About the Author

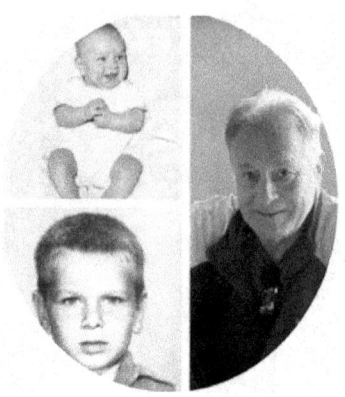

John Harper is a Diamond Approach® teacher, Enneagram guide, and student of human development whose work bridges psychology, spirituality, and deep experiential inquiry. His published books include *Nurturing Essence: A Compass for Essential Parenting*, which invites parents to discover the role essence plays in child development. He is also the author of *The Enneagram World of the Child: Nurturing Resilience and Self-Compassion in Early Life* and *Good Vibrations: Primordial Sounds of Existence*, available on Amazon.

www.ingramcontent.com/pod-product-compliance
Lightning Source LLC
LaVergne TN
LVHW061345060426
835512LV00012B/2565